# THE CHOICE

# THE CHOICE

## PHILLY McMAHON
with Niall Kelly

*Gill Books*

Gill Books
Hume Avenue
Park West
Dublin 12
www.gillbooks.ie

Gill Books is an imprint of M.H. Gill & Co.

978 07171 7913 8

Lyrics from 'Ghosts of Overdoses'
courtesy of Damien Dempsey

Copy-edited by Ruth Mahony
Proofread by Emma Dunne
Print origination by Carole Lynch
Printed by CPI Group (UK) Ltd, Croydon, CRO 4YY

This book is typeset in 13.5/17pt Minion
Title and chapter headings in Frutiger Light

The author and publisher have made every
effort to trace all copyright holders, but if any have
been inadvertently overlooked we would be pleased to
make the necessary arrangement at the first opportunity.

*The paper used in this book comes from the wood pulp of
managed forests. For every tree felled, at least one tree is planted,
thereby renewing natural resources.*

A CIP catalogue record for this book is available
from the British Library.

5 4 3 2 1

*For John*

# CONTENTS

Prologue: 18 September 2011     1

The First Half     9

Half Time     123

The Second Half     159

Epilogue: 1 October 2016     253

# Prologue
## 18 September 2011

I want to stop.

My mind sends the message, but something slows it down as it goes from my brain to my legs. Rust. By the time I jam on the brakes and turn, I've only gone a step or two too far, but that's far enough. It feels like every eye in Croke Park is on me, wondering what's going on, but the reality is that it all happens in a split-second and nobody even notices.

Anyway, they're all watching Colm Cooper as he curls the ball over the bar. The green and gold jerseys are on their feet again.

Fuck. What am I even doing here?

Into the championship rounds and Kerry have their foot on our neck. They're four points up with seven minutes to play, shoulders back and chests out. Two years on, we're not startled earwigs any more, but it's still looking like the same old story. Another chapter in the tale of the nearly men.

A lot of Dubs draw their family tree from roots on Hill 16 and the moments that have been shared there between generations of fathers and sons and mothers and daughters. Standing side by side in their usual spots, they're fighting a losing battle against their worst instincts now and already starting to wonder about what might have been. There's always next year.

There'll be plenty of time for everyone to tell us how we got it wrong. Good but not good enough, they'll say. There for the taking and they couldn't get over the line again. Second best. Maybe that's their level.

I know that Cooper is going to sell me that dummy – there's nothing wrong with how I'm reading the game – but once he cuts in, all I can do is throw out a hand in hope and I'm forced to face the truth. It's mad how deeply you can look inside yourself in those moments, how nothing else registers, even though there are

29 other lads out there fighting with you and against you, and 82,000 spectators hanging on every move. For weeks I've been telling Pat Gilroy that I'm fit and ready, and I've convinced myself, but it's obvious that after two months out injured, I'm an inch or two short of where I need to be. And in an All-Ireland final, inches are the difference between blocks and scores.

But you recognise that and accept it – then you have to forget it. That play is over. When the next ball comes, I'll back myself, same as always. And maybe that's what people don't see when they look at us and they question our heart and our stomach for the battle. This Dublin team has learned its lessons the hard way. Once the final whistle blows, there will be nothing more we can do, but until then, we're not done fighting.

In an instant, everything changes. A quick free from midfield and Alan Brogan is turned and running at them. Kev McManamon is on his shoulder. Give it, give it, give it. Alan waits and pops it but the Kerry men are standing guard. Three of them blocking the path to goal, warning Kev: don't even think about it. He's like me, thrown in from the bench in the second half with only one thing on his mind: make an impact. If he sticks the ball over the bar and gets us back to within three, he'll have done that.

Michael Darragh MacAuley is sprinting through in support. Bernard Brogan is on the edge of the square, crying out for the pass. But Kev is at full tilt and he has other ideas. He drops his shoulder and the goal opens up for him. Then it's all about keeping a cool head.

The Kerry net ripples and the Hill's fading dreams are transformed from a flicker to a roar. Sixteen years those fans have waited for a Dublin All-Ireland, 16 years of doubts and scars wiped away with a goal. A giddiness rushes in to take their place. There are fans my age who can barely remember the glory days of 1995; I barely remember them myself. The Dubs are giants of Gaelic football, for sure, but despite everyone's best efforts, they've been half-asleep for most of my life.

Nobody's nodding off now. The whole stadium is electrified and we're the ones feeding off the energy. Just two minutes earlier we looked tired, nothing left in the tank after an hour of hounding Kerry around the park, and even with that, it looked like we were still going to come up short. Now they're the ones backing up and making mistakes, and we're on the balls of our feet, trying to pick our shots.

Now you'll see what we're about.

We win another turnover and get the ball moving quickly again. Kev Nolan has the freedom of Dublin out on the Hogan Stand side and kicks one of the scores of the day. All square. Then Bernard squeezes over a point to put us into the lead with two minutes left. All around us, the noise and the energy levels have gone up another notch, but the stakes are totally different and there's a nervousness running through it. Hands on heads and on hearts, and then Kieran Donaghy kicks a point to draw Kerry level with 30 seconds to play.

If it goes to a replay, we'll be back here to do it all again in two weeks, but the referee signals that there are two additional minutes to be played and one team is bound to get a chance in that time. We just need to make sure that it's us.

Kev Mc goes down, tripped by a loose leg, and the whistle goes. We have a free, 40 metres from goal, a little to the right of the posts. Kev's still on the ground, hanging onto the ball as if it was the Sam Maguire itself, and they're already waving Stephen Cluxton to come up and kick it. The All-Ireland on the line and he jogs out of his goal past me, the coolest man in the house. All anybody else can do is watch.

As Clucko places the ball, you can't hear the difference between the curses and the prayers. It's all just noise, and it gets louder with each step back that he takes. But then he strikes it, and for a fraction of a moment after the ball leaves his foot, it's like somebody has turned the sound all the way down to zero. A deep breath multiplied by thousands, some in hope and some in fear.

That moment of stillness is so brief that it barely registers before it's swallowed up again. There's a pocket of Dublin fans on the Hill who are in the perfect position to judge the flight of the ball and they're the first to react. It's a sound like nothing I've ever heard in my life, starting from the terrace and wrapping its way around the four sides of the stadium. Defeats in sport don't last forever, but a little bit of every disappointment stays with you, bottled up. Now it's bursting free all around me, uncontrollable joy. The stands shake to their foundations; down on the pitch, it's so loud that my head is shaking too.

We've played the two additional minutes but the game is still not over. Kerry have taken the restart quickly and they're trying to work it down the field. Clucko is sprinting back towards his goal in case they get to within shooting range. I've made the mistake in the past of wishing for a game to be over, and I swore to myself that I'd never let it happen again – but this is every dream I've ever had and it's about to come true.

Blow it up, ref. Blow it up.

He does, and the place erupts all over again. A minute ago, Croke Park was a chessboard, every move on the pitch so precise. Now it's a blur of sky blue and navy, the happiest kind of chaos. We run, even though we've nowhere to run to. We cry, even though we're happier than we've ever been. Arms arrive out of nowhere and pull us into hugs. There are no words, only roars of pure emotion.

By the time we go up to lift the Sam Maguire, I'm banjaxed – not from the game, but from all of the running around and jumping up and down celebrating. I'm sure I'm not the only one.

Michael Darragh gets pulled aside for an interview by RTÉ. I don't know how any player can be expected to explain those feelings, what we could possibly say that would even begin to scratch the surface, but that doesn't stop people from asking. He's buzzing so much he can hardly get the words out. 'Unbelievable,' he keeps saying. 'Unbelievable.' He's right, it is unbelievable – but it'll be a while before we let him live that interview down.

I'm over at the Hogan Stand. I know my parents are in there somewhere, near the Ard Chomhairle box and the steps. I'm scanning through the smiles of different shapes and sizes, every one of them with their own different story about this day and what it means to them.

I find the one I want. It's not difficult. My dad is hard to miss at the best of the times. A big man, and a tough man, and I run to the railings where he's standing, bawling his eyes out. My mam and my sister Kellie are a few rows back, still in their seats, but Dad's made his way down to the front of the stand. In 24 years, I don't think I've ever seen him cry, but he's hugging me and telling me how proud he is, the tears rolling down his face onto my jersey.

Those first few moments are special, just us and our families, before we step out of the bubble and the phones start buzzing and the rest of the world arrives to join the party. This is why we do it. Every hour we put in when we train, every sacrifice we make, it's exhausting – but it's a privilege. We're the lucky ones who get to lace up our boots when everyone is watching, but that Dublin jersey is not ours. It belongs to the communities that shaped us, the clubs that trained us, the families that raised us. Our success will always be theirs too.

Dad eventually lets go of me.

I'm an All-Ireland champion and I'll have these memories forever. It's almost perfect.

All that's missing is John.

# THE FIRST HALF

'Who are you?' he asks me. Good question.

Who do you think I am? An athlete, a Dublin footballer, an All-Ireland winner? A businessman?

Do you think I'm aggressive? A scumbag? A knacker from the flats?

A dickhead? A role model?

Ask me who I am and I'll start with where I come from. I am Ballymun. It is in my blood. It has made me the man I am.

It's where I learned about pride and passion and the importance of hard work. Loyalty. Perseverance.

Love.

And it's where I first discovered that the world we live in has some very sharp edges, and if you're not careful, it's easy to cut yourself.

Prejudice. Poverty. Violence. Crime. Drugs.

Death.

Nobody ever said Ballymun was perfect. Certainly not me. But then, what family is?

Ballymun was supposed to be Dublin's great housing experiment, built from scratch in the 1960s. Thousands of working-class families were living in crowded tenements in the inner city, and the government needed to move them to somewhere else. Anywhere else. They looked out to the north and found empty fields that they could turn into blocks and blocks of high-rise flats. That would be our home. They built four-storey blocks and eight-storey blocks, and, at the heart of it all, the towers: seven of them, each named after one of the seven signatories of the Proclamation of the Republic, 15 storeys of grey concrete stretching out to touch the airplanes that came in to land nearby.

It was sold as the Ireland of the future, a dream with central heating in every flat and lifts in every tower block, but they never built the facilities to make sure that this new community could survive and thrive. For years, there was no shopping centre or library or swimming pool. Instead of shops, we had shop vans, parked up in the fields, to make sure that we could buy our milk and bread and whatever else we needed. It was meant to be a new beginning, but without any support, people struggled to find work and the crime and violence of the inner city found a new feeding ground a couple of miles up the road. When drugs hit Ireland, they hit Ballymun hard. When our problems started to drag us under, the government left us to fend for ourselves until things got so bad that they couldn't ignore us any more.

Somewhere along the way, people stopped seeing Ballymun as a place and started seeing it as a stereotype. A punchline. Ballymunners rob your runners. They forgot that everywhere has its bad parts, and that we were more than just the sum of ours; that for every dealer, there were hundreds of families trying to get by and live their lives; that every tower block with its broken lift and a smell that would knock you back out the door was someone's home.

That's all part of what it means to be from Ballymun – but it's only a black and white version of the colourful, magical place that I grew up in.

Because nothing beat Ballymun on a summer's day. Tops off, walking down the road with the radio on your shoulder, and everybody heading to the same place. We didn't have a beach to go to, and if Ballymun didn't have something, we'd improvise. You could wake up in the morning time and look out your window and there would be 40 stray horses in the field behind our flat. By lunchtime, we'd have turned it into our very own Copacabana. It wasn't just kids or adults, it was everybody. Row after row of sheets, whipped out of the cupboard and laid flat on the ground as beach towels – even in the little things, we made use of what we had and didn't worry too much about the rest. As you walked up along the flats, you'd pass all the different groups, hip hop for some, UB40 for others, some with their bags of cans and plastic bottles of cider, others happy just to lie there and chat and enjoy the good weather. And me in the middle somewhere, kicking a football with John and his mates.

Or if I wasn't kicking a football, I was swinging at a golf ball. Whenever people ask me if I play golf, I say no, because all I can do is use the driver. We'd tee them up in the field and then hit them over the wall into the houses in Glasnevin. They built a wall to divide the two areas, as if being from Ballymun was something bad that you might catch off us if we got too close. The poshie wall, we called it, because once you lived on the other side of it, you were a poshie. Paddy Christie, the Dublin footballer, lived on the other side of the poshie wall. He'd come out of the house to get into his car, and if we were hitting it well that day, a couple of golf balls would bounce down the road past him.

The government forgot about Ballymun. It took them years to build the swimming pool, and once they let us into it, they couldn't get us back out of it. Every Saturday morning, I'd go down with Dad and hand over my money at the desk and get a coloured wristband going in. Hide that. There was a row of coloured lights by the big clock on the wall and once your colour started flashing, it meant your time was up. The buzzer would go off and all the wristbands would instinctively go deeper into the water, 'Ah go on, mister, give us five more minutes,' until they shouted at you to get out, your eyes raw red from the double dose of chlorine they'd used and the smell of it following you around for hours afterwards. Back into the changing rooms, choking on a cloud of Lynx Africa, and you'd get dressed as quickly as you could so that you could get back around to Mannings before the rush. Swimming was always followed by a bag of chester slices, the little cakes made up of dates and raisins and bits of whatever other leftovers were lying around the bakery that morning. Devour them, and if the others were lucky, there might be one or two left by the time we got home.

We didn't have much, but we had the pool hall, where Steo would beat me in a couple of games before the two us went over to Macari's to get a fish box. We had the youth club in the White Elephant, our local community centre. A fashion parade of all the latest Lacoste and Tommy Hilfiger tracksuits and the best of runners, young lads throwing shapes like models from a Brylcreem ad.

We had a community as tightly knit as the smallest village in the country. We didn't need loads of money to have street parties when Ireland were playing in the World Cup or to paint the whole place green, white and orange – the flats, the paths, the poles. We knew each other because we lived on top of each other, six families to a floor in the towers. We shared our lives because there was no other way. Your door was our door and, most of the time, your secrets were our secrets too. When we needed help, we looked to our neighbours, because we knew that we weren't going to get it from anyone else.

We told ourselves that we didn't care about what anyone thought about us, but we did. We wouldn't let the crime or the violence or the drugs define us, and as we carved out our lives so that we could get on with living, our determination brought us closer together. We knew that Ballymun was no ordinary place, that most people didn't have to worry about drug addicts

shooting up in stairwells or pissing outside their front door –
and you were lucky if piss was all it was. We threw down a few
buckets of Jeyes Fluid until the next time and got on with it.
For all of its problems, we were proud of what we had, and it
stung when people talked us down.

If you look at Ballymun from above, with the roundabout at
the centre of everything, it looks very like a Celtic cross – but if
you didn't live there, you wouldn't know the difference between
Balcurris and Balbutcher or Sillogue or Shangan, and who was
feuding with who or why. If you had to cross the Ballymun
Road to go to school, like I did, you needed to know that stuff.
While we were up at the Monos, climbing up on top of the
rocks and jumping from one to the other and throwing
stones at the young lads on the other side of the road, people
who weren't from Ballymun were pushing the speed limit in
their hurry to get in one side and out the other as quickly as
they legally could. They watched TV and read the news – God
knows, the place was on it enough times – and they thought
they knew us.

To an outsider, the flats were the symbol of all of our
problems. They saw young mothers struggling up and down
the stairs of the towers with a buggy and baby in one hand and
an armful of shopping in the other, afraid to even touch off the
rusted handrails for fear of what they might catch. They saw
graffiti on the walls – CAFFO – and boarded-up windows, bin
chutes set on fire for the laugh, kids dodging used needles
hidden in the grass where they played. They saw gangs on the
blocks or addicts coming out of the Redbrick, clutching at their
little bags of carry-out methadone as if it was the only thing
they had in life.

They didn't see Phil and Valerie, who moved around the
corner from the eight-storeys on Sillogue Road to the four-

storeys on Sillogue Avenue so that they would have an extra bedroom and a bit more space for their family when their new baby was born.

They didn't see Ballymun. It was our world.

———

Before I became Philly McMahon, I was Philip Caffrey, but we can come back to that later.

I couldn't tell you who started to call me Philly. It was there from a young age anyway, probably around the time I started to play sport. Philip was just a little bit formal and proper for a young lad in Ballymun. Nobody gets called by their actual name growing up anyway. Look at my mates – Steo, Mossy, Doc, Joycey. And I liked Philly. You might have a go at a kid named Philip, but you would think twice before you started on Philly. Even now, I don't like seeing my name printed as Philip in a match programme. They still do it anyway.

I was named after my dad, Phil. He was born in Belfast at the height of the Troubles. A very proud man, a proud Republican, and a man who had to overcome a lot of adversity in his own life. He moved to Dublin in the 1980s to get away from it all and that's where he fell in love with Valerie.

'Your dad's only a Provo.'

Croke Park is as noisy as you'd expect on a big championship day, so I catch myself to make sure I heard that correctly. The two of us have had a bit of back-and-forth, little pops, nothing unusual. I heard him alright, and he's looking at me now to see how I'll react. Probably hoping that I'll swing for him, that one of the umpires will catch me and see him going down in a heap, and that will be the end of my day. We don't need that.

I am a bit confused though, I have to admit. Am I meant to be embarrassed by that?

The ball is down the other end of the pitch. Neither of us are getting involved in the play at this stage. 'Yeah, is that a bad thing?' I ask him.

Now he's the one on the back foot. Lost focus, lost concentration while he tries to figure out what I'm saying to him, how this trump card he thought he had has backfired.

'What did your da do?' I ask him. 'What did your da do when the Troubles were going on?'

He doesn't have too much more to say for himself after that.

In the back of my head, every time the chips are down for me on the pitch, it's like Dad is there in my ear. He taught me to be resilient, to be tough. Every time there's a setback, I kick on, like he did in life. Slagging my dad isn't going to throw me off my game. It's going to drive me on even more.

I got all of my best qualities from my parents. Mam is a Dub, from Kimmage originally. A southsider, we keep reminding her, although when we start to wind her up for a bit of a laugh the accent goes further and further north until she turns into Belfast Val. Like any Irish son, I could tell stories for days about what an incredible woman she is and the things she did for her five kids: June, Lindy, John, Kellie, and then a gap of three years to me, the baby of the family.

We'd get home from school and the key for the front door would be hidden in the electricity box beside the chute. Mam and Dad would still be out. Mam worked double jobs for a lot of her life, three jobs at times, to make sure that we had everything we needed growing up. The brand of tracksuit that you were wearing, or whether your runners were Nike or Adidas, that mattered to kids in Ballymun.

Mam and Dad always made sure that we had nice clothes, but they also taught us that life is not really about what you have. It's about what you do with what you have.

They raised us to be proud of where we were from. That wasn't always easy in Ballymun, but I never forgot it, and it was only much later in life that I realised how important that was. The path you take in life is influenced by how you see the world and your place in it. It's coloured by the experiences that you've had and, more importantly, the thoughts and stories and meanings that you've created off the back of them. A lot of people who weren't from Ballymun saw the flats and the drugs and the crime and developed a negative meaning around us and our home. We all developed our own meanings too.

Ballymun is where it all started for me. My sport, my businesses, every success I've ever had, you can trace it back to there. Being from Ballymun can be the greatest gift that you ever got in life or it can be a straitjacket. It can raise you up or it can knock you down. Not everybody gets the chance to make something of it. I was lucky. I did.

———

I took one look at the fence and I knew that there was no way that I was getting up and over it without destroying myself on one of the rusty edges sticking out from the top.

'Come on, Philly, just jump it, you'll be grand.'

Just jump it? Easy for you to say when you're twice my size.

A big group of us from Sillogue Avenue were down in the park in Albert College, looking for a bit of mischief if it didn't find us first. Mam and Dad were at work, and June and Lindy weren't around, so it was up to John to look after me for the afternoon. John was a lot of things, but he wasn't a babysitter. I couldn't have cared less, I was just delighted to be able to tag along with him and his mates, safe in the knowledge that he couldn't tell me to get lost or go and hang out with the lads who were my own age.

I always had a bit of a complex about the Caffrey name. It probably came from that stupid schoolyard thing of someone finding a way to twist it into a slag against you, and when it's your name, there's no way to brush it off. As names go, it's a pretty safe one. There's no obvious joke to be made there, but the joke doesn't need to be obvious or even funny for it to get a laugh when you're that age. 'Look at you, you big Caffreys Snowball', or something like that. Slagging me because I shared my name with a little marshmallow cake.

In his group of friends, John was Caffo, so as the little brother, seven years younger, I became Young Caffo. I absolutely idolised John, like any kid does with their big brother. If he had told me black was white, I would have been convinced that the rest of the world had got it all wrong. Being called Young Caffo out on the streets, anything that strengthened that connection between me and John in other people's eyes, that was something that I was really proud of.

John and the lads had scaled the fence, quick as cats, and now they were staring back at me through the chain links, already getting impatient.

'Here, look.'

One of John's mates got a hold of the top of the fence and, hanging off it deadweight, bent it backwards far enough towards the ground that I could manage to get up and over it.

Problem solved – except as I scrambled over, probably more worried about ripping whatever jersey I was wearing, this lad let go of the fence. It sprang back, the edge catching me along the inside of my left arm, ripping it the whole way up along the length of the forearm, palm to elbow.

I must have let some yelp out of me as I hit the ground and the blood started pumping, because the lads started panicking.

'Fuck, give us a look there, Philly. Are you alright?'

John was already gone past panic and straight into damage-limitation mode. He was supposed to be minding me and here I was, the arm half-hanging off me. There was no way he was bringing me home in that state anyway, that's for sure, and there was definitely no way he was telling Mam what had happened if he could avoid it. We always said that John should have been either a lawyer or a politician. He had the number one skill for it: he was great at telling lies.

He got me up off the ground.

'Come on and we'll get this sorted,' he said, the calm in his voice hiding his real feelings.

There's a chemist across from Albert College on the other side of the Ballymun Road, and I'd say they were thrilled to see us coming, a gang of young lads and the youngest one at the head of the party with a strip missing from his arm. To their credit, they were able to sort me out with a few bandages and stop the bleeding for long enough for John to get his story straight and then to get me home again. I'll never forget the look on his face when he walked me in the front door of the flat, pure white as he tried to explain to Mam what was after happening. Even as the words were tumbling out of his mouth, he was still trying to work out what version of the truth would get him in the least trouble.

'Ah, Ma, we were only messing down in the park and he fell, it's grand ...'

Whatever way he tried to pass it off, Mam was having none of it. She took one look at my arm and freaked. Next thing I knew, I was sitting in Temple Street Hospital with an armful of stitches. I still have the scar. It was only years later that we told her the full story.

———

Growing up, every day and night sounded the same: the thump of a football off the wall of the flats, its panels slowly tearing away until I was left with more bare patches than ball and no option except to go down to the shop and buy a new one. As we got older, some lads would be telling stories, others would be having a few drinks, and we'd all be keeping sketch for the guards. But there was always that same soundtrack. The leather on the concrete.

Then we'd get bored or competitive, or both, and the four-storey blocks were just about tall enough to keep us entertained. Stick one man on either side, take a few steps back to give yourself a bit of angle, and launch the ball back and forth over the roof, one side to the other. Or we'd go over to the towers and see how high we could kick it. I don't think I ever got it past the eleventh floor.

You'd be screwed if you misjudged your kick and landed it on top of the roof. Game over, and as well as that, you'd have to buy the new ball – nobody's waiting a couple of weeks for the corpo man to go up there and empty the treasure chest of forgotten footballs. But it was better than having to go and knock on someone's door because it had landed in their window.

Lads dreamed of being the next David Beckham or Robbie Fowler, curling free-kicks into imaginary goals in the chutes. Other fellas just wanted to make friends, and if you could kick a ball, they were always a bit easier to come by.

Me, I picked up a ball because I wanted to spy on John and his friends and see what they were up to.

My big brother was a lot of things. He was smart, even though he never really cared about school. He was kind. He'd give off the impression of being the hard man, but then he'd be the very one doing little things to help other people out.

And he was a messer. Jesus, he was an absolute messer. The seven of us would be squeezed in around the dinner table, and before Mam even had the plates in front of us, John would have us rolling about the place in stitches with whatever funny story he'd heard that day. He was a bit of an entertainer, happy to be the butt of the joke himself if it made people laugh.

I always wanted to be hanging around with him, and he looked after me. We used to go round to the cinema in the shopping centre in Santry. It would be early in the day, still quiet enough in the Omniplex, and John would hand over the tenner that he'd got from Mam or Dad to buy the tickets, all please and thank yous. By the time we got home again, it'd be pitch black outside. The first film might have only lasted two hours or whatever, but there was always a second and a third, and we would be there for the day, skipping from one screen to another, seeing how many different films we could watch for free before we got caught.

When he left school and started working in the Dublin Meat Packers out by the airport in Cloghran, he had his Friday routine. He'd come in the front door, open the envelope, take the first £20 out of his pay packet and hand it to me. His order was always the same and I was ready to go, down to the shop van outside our flat for a tenner's worth of Kinder Buenos, and I could keep a few quid out of the change for myself. I had a sweet tooth growing up – I still do, although I'm pretty good at keeping it in check now – but John's nutrition was absolutely atrocious. If he could have survived eating just fried eggs, chips, and Buenos, that would have suited him fine.

Once a month, he would bring me into town for the afternoon and we wouldn't come home until I'd picked out a new football jersey and he'd bought it for me. It was like having a birthday every few weeks, the two of us bouncing from one sports shop to another and back again, flicking through the racks to see if they'd gotten in any new kits that we hadn't seen before. 'John, look at this one,' I'd say, pulling the away strip of some obscure Italian or French side out of the pile to show him.

I had this amazing collection of different jerseys, but there were only ever two teams that we were allowed to support in our house: Everton and Celtic. They were Dad's teams, and so John became a massive Everton and Celtic fan, and later so did I. Nearly every other kid in Ireland supported either Man United or Liverpool and you'd get some mad funny looks when you told people. That just made it even better for me.

'You support Everton? Why? They're crap.'

John bought me every Everton and Celtic jersey we could find, and loads more others as well. He bought me the only Dublin GAA jersey that I ever owned before I started playing myself, one of the old Arnotts ones from around 2001 or 2002. Even when we both got older and he was living in London, the post would arrive and there'd be an envelope addressed to me with an Everton diary or a match programme that he'd managed to pick up somewhere. A little reminder.

I wasn't the type of kid who got into a lot of scraps. I can't remember ever being in a fight in school, or getting caught up in any of the usual digging matches up at the Monos on the way home. What little fighting I did when I was younger, I saved for the GAA pitch. But like any lad, there were times when trouble found me, even if I hadn't gone looking for it. Given the choice between standing your ground in a scrap or walking away, there was no choice really. When you're brought up in Ballymun, you don't back down. You never back down.

John must have nicked all of the height genes in the family because he shot up into this 6'4" beanpole of a teenager, a big lanky, wiry thing. Bambi, his mates used to call him – all legs and no co-ordination. Bambi was well able to look after himself though, and his little brother too. I got into a scrap with a lad who was a little bit older than me once and let's just say that your man was doing more damage to me than I was doing to him until John arrived on the scene and gave him a clatter. Fight over.

And when your man's da came flying down the stairs to sort things out a few minutes later, John didn't give a shit. He just looked at him. 'Go back up them stairs before I give you a slap as well,' he warned him, and he wasn't messing. The da didn't need to be told twice. His young fella never came near me again.

A lot of the time, John didn't even need to be there in person to protect me. Just mentioning him was enough to make anyone think twice about causing me hassle. 'Get away from me or I'll get my brother to bash you' – those words carried a lot of weight and I wasn't afraid to use them.

It wasn't always a good thing. The two of us shared a room, me on the top bunk, him on the bottom, and inevitably we would end up killing each other, the usual brother stuff. You couldn't even call these things fights. That would imply that there was some sort of contest between us when, in reality, I was like a fly, batted away without a second thought.

I think he was smart enough to know that the tide would turn eventually, and that he wouldn't always have that easy physical advantage over me. His best mate Mick would be hanging around in the flat or the field or wherever, and he'd see these little scraps between us all the time. 'John, see when he gets older,' Mick warned him, 'he's going to batter you.'

There were times when I'm sure I could have, and plenty of times when maybe I wanted to, but I never did.

I would have spent every day and every night following John around if he'd let me, but a lot of the time, he just wanted to be left alone to do his own thing. One Saturday night, Mam and Dad had a few friends into the flat for a few drinks, a couple of the neighbours. I was up to my usual trick, hanging around for long enough until someone called me over and slipped me a few quid for sweets or whatever.

John and Mick landed in. They weren't there for the money, although if you offered it, it would have been gone out of your hand before you knew it. They were more interested in the supplies that our guests had brought over to stock the fridge. A misplaced can would never go unnoticed at the start of the evening, so the lads didn't even chance it, but as the night wore on and people came and went and three drinks became five or was it four, the guard started to slip. John gave Mick the nod to go down the stairs and then whipped a couple of cans, careful not take anything that might be missed, and dropped them over the balcony to him.

It's easy to see why John, 12 or 13 years old and getting his buzz off two cans, didn't want me hanging around. I was a squealer, a little rat. I'd take my ball and go down to near where he was hanging around with his mates and start banging it off the wall. Right foot, left foot, on the volley, off the ground, out of my hands, over and over and over again.

Every so often, I would knock it in their general direction. Never too close to them, but just far enough so that when I went to get it back, I'd get a better look at what they were up to.

And if John was ignoring me, I'd be quick enough to leg it back up to the flat.

'Mam, John's down there with the big lads again and he's drinking beer and he won't play football with me.'

I'd hold out my hand. 'Gimme some money for sweets.'

Like I said, a little rat.

———

The 13 bus goes up Dorset Street and over Drumcondra bridge, and just before it turns left to go down Whitworth Road and out towards Ballymun, you can see Croke Park for a second. I know all of the roads around the ground well, the crowds spilling out of the pubs onto the streets and the Garda escorts leading us through, the blue lights of the motorbike pointing the way for the waves of blue jerseys that just keep coming and coming.

But there were no crowds and no team bus that day. Just me and Mam coming home from town. As we crossed the bridge, I saw Croker and all of its happiness and heartache and heroes and shadows, and I turned to Mam.

'I'm going to play there one day,' I said to her.

You couldn't even call it a statement of ambition, because I hadn't put that much thought into it. Maybe I meant that I'd grow up to become a Dublin footballer and lift Sam Maguire on some of the happiest days of my life. Maybe it wasn't Sam that I was thinking about, but Liam. Or maybe I wasn't even thinking that far down the line, and I knew that in a few weeks' time I'd be lining out there with the hurling team from Holy Spirit National School.

Whatever I meant, it doesn't matter. Mam has never forgotten that day, and never misses an opportunity to remind me of it.

Rewind back a year or two earlier and I wouldn't have been able to tell you where Croke Park was, and the name Sam Maguire would have meant nearly nothing to me. I turned eight in September 1995, a couple of weeks before that great Dublin team drew a line under all of the ifs and buts and gave the county a moment that had been 12 years in the making. It was a scorching hot summer, the summer of Jayo, but I had no real understanding or appreciation of what it all meant.

To be honest, I don't really remember it. Even when a couple of the players brought the cup into our school a few weeks after that Tyrone final, I don't think I was in that day. Thankfully there'd be other chances for me to get my hands on it.

Maybe the buzz around the county got through to me subconsciously, because it was around that time that GAA started to become a part of my world, and to me GAA meant one man. There was a knock on the classroom door and it opened just far enough so that Paddy could stick his head in. Lads nudged each other in their seats, 'Look, there's Paddy Christie.'

Paddy would have only been a teenager himself at the time, on the fringes of the Dublin senior panel and just starting to make his breakthrough, but to the boys of Holy Spirit, he was a superstar, an inter-county footballer living and breathing among us. At first, I didn't know who he was. To me, at nine years old, he was the guy that the other kids were always talking about in the yard. I heard the way they spoke about him, that they had been in the shops with their mam and saw him and said hello and he said hi back, or even better, that they had been to a Dublin match and seen him play, and I knew that he was important. His tracksuit didn't hang off him like ours did when we wore them. He was big and strong, like one of the footballers that we watched and worshipped on TV, except his house was only around the corner and now here he was knocking on the door of our classroom.

'Sorry for disturbing you,' he said to the teacher, 'but can I see the following boys outside for a minute, please?' and then read out a handful of names.

Anyone he called was up out of their seat and outside the door before he had even finished with the rest of his list. They would only be gone for a minute or two, long enough for Paddy to tell them what time training was at or, if it was a Friday, where their match was that weekend and what time they had to meet at, but I was always jealous. Everybody else was talking about Paddy Christie, but these lads were talking *to* Paddy Christie. He knew their names.

He was on a mission and, even though we didn't realise it, we would be his foot-soldiers. I didn't know the first thing about Ballymun Kickhams, but it was Paddy's club and he wasn't going to stand there and watch it all fall apart in front of him while he did nothing. Kickhams were one of the Dublin football powerhouses in the 1980s and, back then, the names rolled off the tongue and onto the team-sheet: Barney Rock, John Kearns, Gerry Hargan, Anto McCaul, all All-Ireland winners. When Paddy looked around, the memories of the two county titles won in 1982 and 1985 were still fresh, but they might as well have happened an eternity ago.

That success had been built on a policy of bringing in local kids and developing them. Frank McCaffrey was a man who had done incredible work to keep the kids' teams in the club going for years, but when he died, a lot of his good work died with him. Bit by bit over the years, the underage structure was allowed to fall away and there were fewer and fewer juvenile teams. Senior teams struggled to find enough players to sustain themselves, and as the older generation retired, there was no hope of fast-tracking young lads through in twos and threes to keep the numbers ticking over. There weren't enough young lads there.

The club lost its way in the 1990s, but as long as its heart was beating there was still a chance, and thankfully there were enough good men and women who refused to give up on Kickhams in those days when things got tough. Men like Paddy Hopkins, who worked day and night to keep young kids from the area involved in the sport.

But holes were still springing up quicker than they could be plugged, and Paddy Christie knew he had to play to his strengths. He wasn't an administrator or a fundraiser or an organiser. He was a coach – so he coached.

To start to rebuild the club from the bottom with a brand new U10s team, he needed players. There were plenty of those in the schools of Ballymun.

All I wanted to do was play sport, and as soon as I was old enough to join a team, I did. I was playing soccer with Ballymun Town, but there was no reason why I couldn't play GAA as well. There were a lot of free hours in the evening after school, and I was never a kid that was going to be too worried about my homework.

I knew which lads from school were going up training with Paddy, and when the summer leagues started, I asked one of them if I could go up to see if I could get a game. If you were interested in GAA, Paddy was interested in you. He told me to come up and see how I got on.

Davey Byrne knocked on the door. Actually, he never knocked – because our flat was on the first floor, he stood at the window and roared.

'PHILLY, ARE YOU RIGHT? COME ON.'

John or whoever leaned out the window. 'Howaya, Davey, he'll be out to you now.'

I legged it out the door, boots in my hand, and the two of us ran to training in Poppintree Park. That was where it all began. Another U10 team started up the following year, and within a few seasons, the underage structure had been completely rebuilt. Years later, when you looked at the Kickhams team that played in the final of the Dublin championship in 2012, you could trace it all the way back to that beginning in the late 1990s. Of the 15 players that started against Kilmacud Crokes that night, 13 of us came from the same U21s side, coached by Paddy, the kind of achievement that will probably never be matched anywhere in the country again.

Back then though, we were just a bunch of eight- and nine-year-olds brought together from opposite sides of the wall. It didn't take much to spot the difference between the lads from Ballymun and the lads from Glasnevin at that age. We were always that bit wilder, making life that bit trickier for Paddy. I was as bad as anyone – I'd say I tortured him. Going to away games, he knew to keep me up at the front of the bus because I'd only be starting a riot if I was down the back.

'Philly, sit in there,' he said to me, pointing into the seat behind the driver where he could keep an eye on me. I'd stopped off in the shops on the way down to get a can of Coke for my breakfast, but I was already hyper before I even had the thing open. We were only on the road for a couple of minutes when I reached up over the headrest in front of me and poured the tiniest drip out of the can and onto the bus driver's head. At least, that was what I meant to do, but I actually ended up pouring most of what was left in the can all over him.

He lost the plot.

'What's that on me bleedin' head?' he shouted, trying to keep his eyes on the road and at the same time work out why the whole bus was roaring their heads laughing. Paddy was going mental beside him. He knew full well who was to blame.

'It was only a bit of water, it was water, I'm sorry,' I stammered, falling over myself trying to explain, but the open can in my hand was a dead giveaway. Even if it wasn't, the fact that the driver's hand was getting stuck to the top of his head when he touched it probably was.

With messing like that, Paddy knew that he had his work cut out for him. He had gathered up a team full of kids from different backgrounds, with different problems, and some of us just didn't like rules or being told what to do or when to do it. Paddy knew that if I had that much energy for messing – and I wasn't the only one – he'd be able to channel that into positive energy on the football pitch.

Those sessions up in Poppintree Park were some of the happiest days of my life. If I could have stayed there all night, I would have. The type of football that Paddy taught us was very much in his image: tough, quick, and skilful. He'd show up at training with this big pocket full of change, and at the end of each session, he'd pick a skill that he wanted us to work on.

The whistle blew. 'Right, we're finishing off with shooting. Everyone grab a ball and go out to those red cones.'

When we got to the cones, we noticed that they were a couple of yards further back than we were used to, or at a little bit more of an angle. It was a competition, miss and you're out. We took it so seriously. You wouldn't see that pressure on a kick in an All-Ireland final – lads making sure that every blade of grass was arranged to prop the ball up before they'd even dream of taking their shot. The winner always got a pound coin from Paddy at the end, which was a little thing, but it got us to concentrate and work hard and kept us coming back for more.

When we were getting changed after a match, Paddy would announce his man of the match. That was worth two or three quid to the winner so we'd all be looking around, wondering who it was going to be. He was smart about it. If he felt that a certain player had more to give or that they had taken their eye off the ball a bit, he'd pick somebody who was fighting for that spot or playing in a similar position and he'd give them man of the match instead. Again, it was something really simple, but it showed that he understood how to keep us interested and bring the best out of us.

The other thing about Paddy is that he is a person who thinks before he speaks. He knows the impact that his words can have on the kids that he's coaching, and he's very careful in how he chooses them.

After my team had all moved out of underage and on to senior level, Paddy went back and he started again with a brand new group of U10s. There's a young lad, Aaron Elliott, who would have been part of that second wave and he's playing senior with us now and involved in the Dublin underage squads as well.

There was one day when they had a championship match, and Aaron arrived into the dressing room a few minutes late.

'Aaron, what's the story? You're late.' Unusually for Paddy, he jumped straight in without thinking and went through him so quickly that he didn't even notice that Aaron had limped in, dragging his leg behind him.

Aaron was a bit taken aback by Paddy's reaction, but knowing the lad, he just wanted to get on with getting ready.

'Yeah, sorry, Paddy,' he explained. 'I got hit by a car there on the way up, but I'm grand, it's just a bit sore.'

He had been hit by car and was still there in the dressing room, ready to get togged off. He wasn't even particularly late, if we're being honest. Paddy tells that story to make the point: always think about the situation for a second before you speak because the obvious explanation might not be the right one.

He uses it too to give other lads a bit of a kick up the hole from time to time – if a guy like Aaron Elliott can get knocked down and still show up and play a match, the rest of you can at least make it to training on time.

There were a couple of lads that Paddy took under his wing, and myself and Davey were definitely two of them.

'Where were yous tonight?' The sun was just going down behind the towers, but the lads were still out hanging around, and they were always curious. Myself and Davey had been gone for a couple of hours and we were only getting back now.

'What?'

'Where were yis?'

'Ah, we were up at the match with Paddy Christie.' There wasn't much they could say now to cut the legs out from under us.

A couple of times a week, the two of us would walk around and jump the wall into Glasnevin and knock over to his house, where there'd usually be a nice sports car sitting outside in the driveway. I looked at Paddy, the coolest person I knew, living in the good houses, driving the big fancy car, and I must have thought that GAA was a professional sport. How else could he have all these nice things?

Paddy would come out, gear bag on his shoulder, and we'd pile into the back of the car and he'd drive us up across the M50 to Páirc Ciceam in Collinstown. When we were kids, it was still a work in progress. There were two big pitches running lengthways and two Portakabins as dressing rooms, and that was it. Over the years it has transformed into one of the best club facilities in the country, thanks to the hard work of men like Val Andrews, who fought to get a full-sized all-weather pitch built at a time when it was totally unheard of in the GAA, but it was bare bones starting out.

Paddy would be going to his own training session with the senior team or to a match, and he'd bring me and Davey up with him to run around as ball-boys or pick up cones or carry the bags. It meant we had somewhere to be on the couple of evenings a week when we weren't at training ourselves. More than that, Paddy was putting us into the environment that he eventually wanted us to be part of. Me and Davey would sit in the senior dressing room before throw-in and watch these men that we worshipped. We'd look at the boots they were wearing and how they strapped up their injuries, smell the Deep Heat. We'd listen to their jokes and to the passion in their team-talks, and the two of us would feel like we belonged. That was Paddy's greatest stroke of genius: opening our eyes and making us realise that, one day, we could be the ones sitting there in the red and green jersey. That was something to dream about, to chase and aspire to, and he was always subtly reinforcing the idea that if we wanted it for ourselves, there was nothing stopping us from going and getting it.

Paddy planted the first seeds of the Dublin dream as well. If he wasn't involved in the squad for whatever reason, he would round up a gang of us and bring us to the match. The days when he was playing himself, there would always be a bundle of tickets left for whoever wanted them. Then when he was handing out the team awards at the end of the season, he would have a load of his own Dublin gear to give to the winners. You can imagine the excitement for whoever had won – that's Paddy Christie's jersey or gloves. As the prize was handed over, there was always that unspoken message as well: if you're ready to go and fight for it, some day you'll be playing for Dublin yourself.

The message got through. You only have to look at the list of lads from our team who went on to play senior inter-county football at one stage or another – me, Davey, Sean Currie, Alan

Hubbard, Jay Whelan, Ted Furman, Elliott Reilly – and then Dean Rock and James McCarthy, who were a couple of years younger but joined us at U21s. It is a phenomenal return and Paddy showed us the way.

———

There was never much crossover between my different groups of friends and the different sports. When I started out playing GAA, most of the lads that I hung around with at home played for Setanta, the hurling club on the Ballymun Road. I played a bit myself, on and off, until I was 14 or 15, but by that stage Kickhams and football came first.

The lads who played soccer were a different group again, for the most part. Soccer was always big in Ballymun, whether it was people going down to watch Ballymun United in the San Siro – which got its nickname from Milan's famous stadium because it was penned in on all four sides by the flats of Balcurris and Balbutcher – or the five-a-side tournament in Poppintree Park that Dympna Doolan organised every year between all the different areas.

I'd come in from school, throw my bag of books down in the hall and run into where Dad was sitting in his big chair.

'Can we go and practise my headers please, Da?'

We spent hours in the field at the back of the flats, making up little games and competitions to see how many I could get in a row, header after header after header after header. Other days, I'd be so tired coming in from school that I'd just climb up on his lap and fall asleep on top of him while he sat there watching telly.

John had no real interest in kicking the ball about, but there were plenty of lads around Sillogue who did. There were always games on the five-a-side pitch underneath the tower block, Sillogue Avenue v Sillogue Road, or we'd arrange little tournaments among ourselves in the field.

'Move it a bit quicker, Philly.'

That was Billy, our 'manager'. He'd get a group of us together for those tournaments, pick the team and tell us what positions to play in. He was a couple of years older than us, but he came down because he wanted to watch his younger brother play and, mainly, you would suspect, because he loved football. I tried to be like Billy, copying the things he did when he passed the ball and shot. He was one of the most naturally gifted athletes I think I've ever come across.

It didn't matter what sport it was or who he was up against, he was inevitably in a different class to everyone else on the pitch. Years later when I got to know Bernard Brogan playing for Dublin, he asked me, 'Did you know Billy?' Word about his skills obviously spread as far as the Navan Road anyway.

Ballymun Town was the first team I ever joined. We got ready for our matches in the basement of the flats: flickering lights, no windows and dust hanging in the air forever as we peeled the dried muck off our boots. Dublin Corporation had decided that it wasn't fit for anything else, but it was good enough to be the dressing room for a group of seven- and eight-year-olds. It was that or nothing, take it or leave it.

Alby Jenkins walked in with a bag full of jerseys. He threw one to me: 'Philly, centre-midfield'. Alby was one of the heartbeats of schoolboy football in Ballymun. People like him get taken for granted a lot of the time, especially by the kids around them who don't know any better, but that club only existed because of his commitment. He'd seen it all before, and he knew that we needed sport at a young age to give us an outlet and focus that would have been totally missing from our lives otherwise. When I was 13, I left to join Belvedere for a season, and by the time I came back, Ballymun Town had merged with Ballymun United. Alby was still there with the balls and bibs a couple of nights a week and every weekend. I owe him a huge amount.

Saturday mornings started a little bit earlier when I moved to Belvo. Three or four times a week, I jumped into the front seat of the car where Mam was already waiting for me, her book or magazine sitting on the dashboard. Ballymun Town's pitch was on our doorstep in Sillogue, but Belvedere were based down in Fairview Park and you couldn't let a 13-year-old, no matter how streetwise, make his own way there and back. Mam drove down and sat there for hours, reading and waiting until I was done and it was time to go home again. The days when we didn't have the car, Dad walked me down and back to the park, a bit more than a two-hour round trip.

I left Belvedere as a much better footballer than they had found me. They're a phenomenal club, and I'm still involved doing a little bit of training with their schoolboy teams, but there was a lot of pressure on us to play well and win every week. With Ballymun Kickhams, Paddy made us feel like little superstars. He arrived down to training with armfuls of Adidas kitbags and Puma runners and boots, a little touch that made us feel that we were involved in something special. At Belvedere, it was so competitive and the coaches were so driven that we were always looking over our shoulders. I needed more carrot than stick.

Leaving Belvo to go back to Ballymun United was a drop down in level – I think we were playing in the third division – but I was happy to be back playing ball with my mates: Rog, Deco, Keith Caulfield, Bob Keating. In a way, I stood out even more when I went back. I was tough and fit, and as much as I loved a tackle, I loved a pass even more, dropping off a bit behind the midfield and trying to pick out a man on the opposite side of the pitch. I just loved whacking the ball. Marc Hartigan was our centre-half, like a young Rio Ferdinand, fast, impossible to get by. He lived up the road in Poppintree and I knew him from the Comp – Trinity Comprehensive, our secondary school.

We were playing good football, and we were at that age where scouts start to pay a bit of attention. Ballymun United had been around since the late sixties and, as far as I know, nobody from the club had ever been away on trial. Now there were two or three scouts a game coming down to our matches. You're looking forward to every game because you know that there's someone watching that can help you get to England.

It became an obsession. Instead of hanging around with our friends, Alby had me and Marc down in Poppintree Park every night for two or three months, just the three of us, when everyone else had gone home.

He checked his watch. 'Last one, lads, let's go.'

Deep breaths, the sweat rolling off the both of us, and we pushed hard to the end of that last drill. This was a man with a family and a life of his own, and for those couple of months, he gave everything to make sure that we got our shot in England, and that if we didn't, we could never look back in later life with regrets and say that we threw away our chance because of a lack of desire or effort.

The call from Nottingham Forest came in a funny way. One of the referees who did a lot of our games noticed that we had a bit of something about us and he told his brother, who was one of Forest's spotters in Ireland. Whatever it was that the two of us were doing well, we kept doing it when the scouts came down to watch us. It was enough to convince them that Marc and I both deserved another look. The plan was to bring us up to Northern Ireland as part of a Forest team for the Milk Cup, where we'd be playing against some of the biggest clubs from around the world. Manchester United, Barcelona, Bayern Munich – they're the kind of names that you'd see at the Milk Cup. It would have been incredible but, whatever way the dates fell, it wasn't possible. Instead, they took us over to Nottingham for a week.

Expectations change, and even if people aren't getting carried away, they start to see you differently. I wasn't just another 14-year-old headwrecker that looked like he was about to cause trouble at the drop of a hat; I was the 14-year-old that was going over to England. I started to see myself differently too. My friends talked about becoming a professional footballer like it was a dream, but maybe this could be my life. 'Golden Balls', John and the girls started to call me, just like Beckham.

There was excitement in school, sport being on the short list of things that can get teenage boys to show any hint of interest. There was always that little bit of jealousy as well, unspoken most of the time but there, ready to be used as a weapon if a fight broke out. I got into a row with a lad, a very good friend of mine actually, and we had a right go slagging each other.

'You think you're great going over to Nottingham Forest,' he shouted. 'You're not even going to make it.'

So much for thinking that everyone wanted you to do well. It's that thing of never letting anyone get too big for their boots, and we start them young here in Ireland. I brushed it off.

'Yeah, well at least I got a trial. You didn't.'

———

The coach from Forest got onto the bus and started doing the rounds to introduce himself to everybody.

He got to me and stuck out his hand.

'Heya, I'm Philly,' I said, sitting up straight in my seat in case he was already sizing me up. Too small, too slight, does he have the pace?

'I know who you are,' he said, shaking my hand. 'I've watched a video of you playing.'

He quickly moved on to the other lads but my head was spinning. Hold on a second – if they've been taping you and watching it already, that's serious, isn't it? Forest had been in the Premiership a couple of seasons earlier, in the late 1990s, but now they were back in the First Division, or the Championship as it's known these days. The stars that they'd had, big names like Pierre van Hooijdonk, had moved on, but they were still getting crowds of around 20,000 at a game. Another young Dub, Andy Reid, was just starting to nail down his place in the first team.

When we got to Nottingham, they put us up in Trent Bridge Cricket Ground, right across the road from Forest's own stadium, the City Ground. It was like that ad where the guy wakes up and he opens the door and there's a stadium right there on his doorstep. We woke up in the mornings, opened the sliding doors, and walked out into the cricket stadium. Unreal.

We did two or three days of training as a group, some shape work and some skills, and then at the end of it we had two matches, against a team from America and a team from Mexico. As much as the coaches were trying to assess our skills, I think they wanted to see if we had the discipline to make it in a youth team. They gave us these guidelines at the start of the week, laying down their rules and letting us know exactly what was expected of us. If we couldn't match up to the basics, really simple stuff like tucking your T-shirt into your knicks when you're training, we had no chance of making it.

One of the mornings, the head of the Forest academy came down to run his eye over us and who was there running around with his T-shirt hanging out? In my defence, I wasn't the only one. He didn't say a word, but I knew he had noticed. Two minutes later, one of the coaches who was taking the session was straight over to us, fuming. By that stage, I was at least smart enough to have tucked my T-shirt back in.

'What are the rules about your T-shirts?' He didn't find this the least bit funny. 'Who had their T-shirt out?' he asked.

Silence, as a couple of lads seemed to take an unusual interest in examining the instep of their boots.

A lad from Dublin that we didn't know piped up. 'Him,' he said, pointing his finger directly at me.

I was straight down on the ground, 10 press-ups as my punishment, and in my head I was absolutely fuming. I knew this was competitive, but do it on the pitch – don't go grassing on another lad over something tiny like an untucked T-shirt. The fact that this was another Irish lad, another Dublin lad, only made it even worse.

In the evenings, the coaches brought us out for a bit of food and to show us around Nottingham. The night before one of our matches, we were sitting down getting pizza, but we were told: no fizzy drinks before your match tomorrow. Well didn't I see my pal, the little T-shirt inspector coach's pet, slurping away on a can of Coke down the other end of the table? I was on it like a flash.

'Eh, I thought you said we weren't allowed have fizzy drinks,' I shouted over to the coach. 'He's drinking Coke.' Your man was caught rapid, it was hilarious. That'll teach you to rat me out.

Another morning, the coach pulled myself and Marc to one side at the very start of the session.

'Go up and grab the gear bags there and bring them down,' he said.

Myself and Marc just looked at each other, and it was obvious that the two of us were thinking the exact same thing. The two of us legged it up to the room and there were a couple of big bags of lovely Forest gear, a long-sleeved white Umbro jersey and knicks and socks and the rest.

Marc didn't even need to say it, but he did anyway. 'Here, Philly, will we grab a bit of stuff here?'

I was already rooting through the bag looking for my size. 'Listen,' I said to him, 'if we don't get called back over again, at least we'll have a load of nice gear.'

I got a full kit and stuck it in my own bag, Marc did the same, and the two of us slung the two big gear bags over our shoulders and bounced down the stairs grinning from ear to ear to hand them over to the coaches. Nobody ever found out, nothing was ever said. That white jersey is still at home somewhere.

England was in the middle of a heatwave that week, and the pitches we were playing on were like concrete. I wore studs in our first game against the Americans and I limped off the pitch. My feet were in shreds, covered in blisters.

I played in both games, against the American Cubs, who were basically an American All-Star team, and the following day against a club from Mexico. I thought I played well, but it's difficult. You've got a team made up of triallists who think that this is their dream on the line, and everyone is trying to do their own thing to show off and hopefully catch the coaches' eye. It makes it nearly impossible to play together as a team and if you're playing in centre-midfield like I was, trying to just knit everything together, it's very difficult to stand out from the crowd. The coaches are watching and they know that it's an investment to bring you over from Ireland. You really have to be a cut above everyone else and give them no option but to bite the bullet.

When we woke up on the morning of the second game, it was even hotter, the sun absolutely thumping down and draining all of the energy out of us, and we were trying to keep up with these Mexican lads. They were flying around the place, well used to the heat and not a bother on them, and we were looking after them with our tongues hanging out of our mouths. Thankfully, somebody had the sense to realise that we'd never be able to play two halves of football straight through in those temperatures, so they let us take a couple of water breaks. At half time, there was a massive big bucket over on the sideline and I was straight over to it, sticking my head into it to try to cool down a little bit.

There was one moment in that game when I thought I was maybe after doing enough to make a good impression. One of their lads had the ball and was flying down the sideline. I was coming across to cover and I was determined that he wasn't going to beat me. He was going at some speed so the window to get my timing right was a small one. I flew into the tackle and got the toe of my boot on the ball, while at the same time absolutely milling through your man and putting him up in the air. The head academy guy was standing on the sideline right in front of us, and as I jumped back to my feet and dusted myself off, I could see a little smile on his face. Well done, great tackle.

It wasn't enough to get them interested. At the end of the five days, the coaches took us up into this office to give us either the good or the bad news. I sat there in a chair three times too big for me, hoping, but it wasn't a particularly long conversation. 'We're not going to take you back over,' he said, like a robot programmed to repeat the same phrases on a loop.

'But we'll be looking out for you over the next year or two to see how you develop.'

It's quite a harsh system, years of fighting to get noticed and then, when you do get your shot, you've got a couple of training sessions and two games to make the impression of a lifetime. I would have loved to get called back over for a second trial a year or two later. Going over at 14 was far too young, and I've always felt that if I had got the call and gone over at 16 or 17 instead, I would have been a much more developed, much smarter footballer. I was too inexperienced and immature to realise that there might not be a second chance at it. I know I didn't play to my potential, definitely not, and if things hadn't panned out for me the way they did with Dublin a few years later, it would probably be something that I look back on with a bit of regret.

The curiosity is still there though, the wonder that if I had got a second shot at Forest or at somewhere else, would I have made it?

————

'**M**a, can I go to the beach with Steo and them?' It was one of those magical Ballymun days, a scorcher, and there was a gang getting ready to go out to Killiney: Steo, his brother, his brother's girlfriend, and a couple of the nephews. I had never been to Killiney before – I'd barely been on the southside – and I didn't want to miss it.

'Go on, yeah, just be careful,' Mam said, looking for her purse to give me a few quid for the train and for an ice-cream.

The beach was absolutely packed when we got out there, and the waves were amazing, big huge ones that you could dive through or just lie there and let them pick you up and carry you back closer to the shore. It was so simple, but it is an incredible memory. We have a photo from that day with all of us in it. One of the guys in it was still very young when he died of an overdose a couple of years later.

Every so often in Ballymun you get memories of people that were associated with you, a friend or people you know of, and they've got caught up in drugs and addiction, and died. That's the tough part. You have to try to remember the good times.

Steo is still one of my best mates. He lived in the flats around the corner and hung around with the lads from Sillogue Road. There was no turf war between them and our lads from Sillogue Avenue or anything, just two different groups of friends, but the two of us got on great.

He was probably the only redhead in Ballymun that you wouldn't dream of slagging, not because he'd bash you, but because he'd cut you in half with the slagging you'd get back. He had that quick wit and a mouth to match it. It wasn't just out on the street that he was smart either. He was really intelligent, brilliant in school while the rest of us were hardly bothered doing a tap.

And even though he was always in the top class, he was still a bit mad. There was this massive bang over in the Comp one day, it sounded like a bomb was after going off in one of the classrooms, and next thing you know Steo was being marched down to the principal's office, the rest of the box of bangers still in his hand. He was brilliant at pool too, played for Ireland, and we spent enough time hanging around the snooker hall up at the shopping centre that some of his good habits were bound to rub off on me.

When the rest of the lads hit 13 or 14 and started drinking, me and Steo became even closer friends because we didn't drink. I still don't – never have, apart from a mouthful of lukewarm Bulmers I had one night out in the field. All of the sport I was playing obviously helped to keep me away from the temptation of that kind of messing at a young age, but more than that, I just thought it was rank.

'Do you like this?' I said, the lads watching me for a reaction as I thought about spitting it back out. 'It's mouldy.'

I've always been the kind of person that if I don't like something, I don't bother doing it. Me and Steo certainly didn't need alcohol to be having the craic and getting up to all sorts. The rest of the lads just accepted it, though they'd still try to wind you up a little bit.

When I was 16, we went to Crete, the first time I was allowed to go away with all my mates. I was a good bit younger than most of them. As soon as we arrived in Hersonissos, the lads were straight into this bar, Players. They were handing out flyers for two-for-one drinks outside, trying to get people in, and that was the lads sold for the rest of the holidays.

The gag was always the same. Someone would go up to the bar and come back with their two drinks and put one down in front of me.

'That's yours, Philly. I got you a drink.'

Then there'd be a pause for a second.

'Ah you don't want it, grand,' and he'd reach over, pick it up, and lash it back himself.

They'd try to sneak a bit of whiskey or vodka into my Coke for the laugh, but if one of them handed me a soft drink, I knew well enough to sniff it before I started drinking it.

Over the years, I got more and more enjoyment out of people coming up to me at parties or nights out or whatever and saying, 'You don't drink? You look like the drunk person, you're dancing that much and having that much craic.' Or my mates saying, 'The way you go on when you don't drink, I can't imagine what you'd be like if you did.'

What do I drink? I drink water. I've enough of a buzz going on without anything stronger.

———

I never had the balls to rob anything – the kit I stole from Nottingham Forest that time was an exception rather than the rule – but the lads I hung around with were absolutely fearless. They would walk into somebody's garden, pick up a bike, put it on their shoulder, and walk back down the road as if it was the most natural thing in the world. Part of it was for mischief and part of it was for money, and a lot of the time, it was a progression from one to the other. It usually started with something small at a young age, and out of boredom more than anything else. If you didn't play sport, there was really nothing else for you to do growing up in Ballymun. Lads weren't exactly inside watching *Glenroe* and finishing their homework on a Sunday night. You hung around the flats and waited for something to happen.

None of us are born into a vacuum. You might hear your parents talk about how some people look down on them because they're from Ballymun, or an older brother or a sister comes home and says, 'I didn't get that job because I'm from Ballymun,' and subconsciously, it all filters through, that feeling that you've already been pushed out to the edge of society and you haven't even started to live your own life yet. It's hard to see how you could be any different, why anybody would give you a chance.

You start to see the world as a place of no jobs, no opportunities, no diversion. When you feel that there's nothing at risk and you've nothing to lose, there isn't really the same fear of getting caught committing petty crime. There aren't the same consequences. You're playing at a different table with different stakes; it's not even the same deck of cards.

There was always a mix of ages in the groups we hung around with, and inevitably the younger lads would see what the older lads were doing and start to copy them, or the older lads would get them involved to help. There was one little fella, and I don't know how this particular talent was discovered, but he was able to put his hand up underneath the cash register in a shop and take the money out of the till. Four or five of the older lads would go into the shop with him and they'd split up, distracting the security guard while the young lad emptied the notes from the till. If anyone got caught, there were enough of them there that security wouldn't know who to go for first or what to do. They must have stolen thousands of euro doing the same thing in different shops all around Dublin.

In that environment, all it took was for somebody to show you, 'Look, I robbed this and made loads of money,' or, 'Look, I took this drug and it was great,' and all of the rest would jump on board. There were no resources for young people who had taken the first steps down that wrong path, or anyone who was at a high risk of following them. There was nothing.

I didn't get involved because I didn't get invited. I was off at training, either soccer or GAA, or playing a match, putting everything I had into getting better and getting noticed, whether that was for another trial in England or for one of the Dublin development squads. The times when I was around, they knew I'd be useless and probably just get caught.

There was one time though, when they must have been stuck because they needed me. They could see I was a bit uneasy about the whole thing.

'Ah lads, I dunno …'

'For fuck's sake, Philly, just go over there and stand at the bus stop as if you're getting a bus. It's not hard.'

The Garda station has moved now but it used to be connected to the shopping centre, with The Towers pub right beside the guards. The pub had a little small outdoor part to it up on the second floor and, if you knew what you were at, you could get down into the backyard of the station. The guards were taking any motorbikes that were robbed that they'd managed to recover and putting them in the back of the station, and lads were jumping down over the wall to rob them back. They'd break the lock with a Bullsnips and drive the bike straight back out the gate. I had the easy job – stand at the bus stop across the road and keep sketch in case a patrol car pulled up.

No sooner than the lads had got over the wall, the guards arrived back at the station. Oh bollocks. I whistled, loud enough so that the lads could hear me, which was also loud enough so that the guards could hear me. The car door opened and one of them came straight for me, while the other went into the station.

'What are you whistling at?'

Oh fuck, what am I going to say here?

'Ehhhhhh, my mate's just gone over there,' I said, pointing vaguely in the direction of the shops. I thought I was being smart, as if the guards had never heard an excuse like that before.

He knew exactly what was going on.

'You can't be hanging around there,' he said to me. 'Go on off home.' By that stage, they'd already caught one of the lads as he tried to get back over the wall with a bike.

That was the closest I ever came to getting in any trouble with the guards. One of the things Dad always told me was never bring trouble home to your door, and I knew better than to test him on that. He wouldn't even need to raise his hand to you because once you heard that big, strong northern voice, you knew that you were after crossing the line.

One summer the lads decided that they were going to rob a bike – not just any old motorbike this time. A superbike. A huge gang of them went off one day to God knows where and came back a couple of hours later with this absolute beauty of a machine. It must have cost a fortune.

These lads all knew how to drive a motorbike, but I hadn't a clue, I'd never been on one in my life. The only thing I'd ever driven was the petrol scooter that I had begged and begged Mam and Dad to get me. I must have had them tortured over it because it cost around £400, which they definitely didn't have spare, and they went out and bought it for me anyway. I was one of the first kids to get one in the area, certainly the first out of my group of friends, and I thought I owned the place, flying up and down the road. The noise would go through you, you'd nearly need earplugs, but I loved it.

The lads had all had their go on this big superbike and I was the last one. I got on it, after some persuasion, and I nearly killed myself. You'd wonder how I didn't get into trouble, bombing around the field in Ballymun on a stolen motorbike, even if it was only for a minute, but I was lucky, and I was so stressed by it that I learned my lesson after that.

They got rid of the bike a little while later, sold it on – or at least, they tried to. They sent a message to another gang down the road to see if they wanted to buy it, and those lads were interested. Price agreed, deal done. They stuck one of the young lads on the bike and got him to drive it down, collect the money, and come back. Nobody saw the very obvious flaw in this plan, but it shouldn't have come as a surprise when the gang lifted the kid off the bike, gave him a hiding for his trouble, and sent him on his way with no money. If our lads wanted to get paid, they'd have to go looking for it. That was the start of the feud between Sillogue and Shangan.

When my friends first started taking drugs, it happened in much the same way, out of a combination of boredom, peer pressure, and a general acceptance that they had nothing much to lose by trying them. Accessibility too. I knew all the drug dealers in Ballymun. I knew most of their names, what they sold, and who they sold to. I knew the blocks they lived in, the blocks they dealt on, and where they hid their stash. I knew where my friends got their drugs, and if I ever wanted to buy some for myself, I would have known how to get them. Everyone did.

Heroin ripped through Dublin in the 1980s and 1990s, and this place we loved was at the heart of the city's epidemic. The veins of addiction scattered out from it and drew even more problems to us. Our homes were places where dealers could become very wealthy, and we were the ones who paid the price.

Drugs were sold all around us – in front of the flats, outside the shops, inside the shops, on the way home from school. When the 36 bus pulled up on the main road, we could spot the addicts as they got off, coming from all over the city to get their fix. Young children knew to look out for dirty needles where they played and knew not to touch them. The stairwells of the blocks were like a revolving door, addicts going to or coming from their dealer's flat, or worse, using right there in front of you, slumped with a syringe in their arm, so consumed that they didn't care who noticed.

We saw the blue lights of ambulances and heard stories of people found dead from overdoses. We knew neighbours who suffered so much that they stepped off the balconies of the flats and ended their own lives.

The problem was hidden in plain sight. Occasionally – but not as often as you'd think – two or three cars would come from nowhere and pull up at the bottom of one of the towers, and the guards would pile out and into the building. They wouldn't have been hanging around to wait for the lift, even if by some miracle it was working, and there are enough stairs in one of those towers. A smart dealer would hear the commotion long before the guards burst through the door and, if they were lucky, would have enough time to get rid of whatever they had on them.

One of the nights after a raid, we were walking by the same block a little bit later and one of the lads stopped to bend down and pick something up. It looked like he was going to tie his shoelace, but when he stood back up, he had a little bag in his hand.

'Lads, look at this,' he said, waving the heroin in front of us with a smile on his face.

He had no intention of using it himself. In his mind, he'd just stumbled on a quick payday, not realising that it had been thrown out the window in a panic during the raid. We hung around the blocks for a while until he spotted one of the dealers coming down from the tower. He was over to him like a light.

'Here, I have this,' he said, taking the bag out of his pocket. 'Do you want to buy it off me?'

It was gone out of his hand as quickly as it appeared.

'Gimme that. Where the fuck did you get that? That's mine.'

He was lucky that he got away with a few slaps. It could have been worse.

When drugs flooded into Ballymun, nobody was exempt from the problem and nobody was immune from the pain. We were always close as a community – you don't have much choice when you're clustered together in high-rise flats – but we couldn't have built our lives in any other way. Our nearest neighbours and friends might as well have been aunts and uncles. If Mam and Dad were out at work and any of us needed something, we knew that we could knock upstairs to Joan McDaid and she would look after us. Dinner could be anywhere, and equally, anyone could show up and we'd squeeze in an eighth or ninth chair somewhere around our table. If you were out playing on the blocks and Mossy asked if you were hungry, you didn't say no. His dad was a chef and whatever way his mam made those unbelievable roast potatoes, she might as well have been one too. Mossy would go in the door and give her a big kiss. 'Can Philly stay for dinner with us, Mam?' The answer was always yes, and it was always incredible.

But we needed each other for more than friendship. Our lives were never going to be lived in straight lines, and we relied on each other for help and support so that we could find a way to get through the day and get on to the next one. Every family wasn't best friends, there were rows and disagreements, but we knew that if we didn't look out for each other and the little that we did have, nobody else would. Our problems didn't drive us apart. When they were at their worst, that's when we pulled together tightest.

Drugs had no place in our Ballymun, and we were the only ones who were willing to fight for it. We marched. The crowd would come down the street and sweep you along with them. It was like playing Snake on the old Nokia phones, walking through all of the different areas and estates and the rally getting bigger and bigger as more and more people joined on to it.

And the call and response.

'WHAT DO WE WANT?'

'PUSHERS OUT.'

'WHEN DO WE WANT IT?'

'NOW.'

That type of vigilante activism, the people taking the law into their own hands, was a last resort, but it was effective. A lot of dealers were forced out of the community.

But still the drugs came.

―――

It was only when I started playing sport and travelling to away games that my eyes were really opened to the negativity surrounding Ballymun. I loved where I was from, and I'd defend it to the death, but these people just wanted to write us off.

'Yis scumbags.'

'Knackers.'

'Go back to the flats.'

We were 14.

And we were grown men. We were still getting the same narrow-minded bullshit only two or three years ago. I won't name and shame the club, but they are from an upper-class part of the city. We won the match, but it had been spiky enough, and there was a little bit of afters. Some lads wanted to shake hands, others wanted to get involved in a bit of pushing and shoving, and as the teams came together in the middle of the pitch, their manager shouted, 'Go back to the flats.'

Whatever had gone on before, that was like putting a lit match to the lads and a couple of them went berserk trying to get after him. You can maybe make some excuses when kids say stupid things, but this was a grown man and his first instinct was to reach for the symbol of everything that we loved and throw 'the flats' at us like some sort of dirty word. Never mind that the towers didn't even exist any more – they had already been knocked down.

I wasn't playing that day, but I was close enough to see that the little bit of daylight between our lads and theirs was getting narrower and narrower. There weren't going to be any handshakes now. I grabbed the manager and pulled him to the side. I think it might have already been dawning on him that he had made a mistake.

'Listen, that was the wrong thing to say to these lads,' I said to him. 'You can't be saying that stuff. You need to make it right.'

He apologised and, immediately, you could see our lads take a step away. They were still furious, but there was no need to be holding each other back and there wasn't going to be a row. They made sure they got their point across, but it didn't get any more serious than a few raised voices. There might even have been a handshake or two at the end.

I was happy with how I handled the whole situation myself. The lads were looking for blood, but I think it made an impression – hold on, if Philly's not having a go at this guy, then neither should we.

Philly McMahon, the peacemaker. That has a nice ring to it.

As kids, our reputation preceded us. Teams heard the name and they arrived up nearly expecting us to box the head off them. They came in past the flats on their way to the pitch, maybe saw a couple of young lads taking their ponies out for a trot in the field, and their stomachs began to tighten that little bit. We weren't a rough team though. Were we tough? We thought so. Were there fights? Obviously. But we weren't nasty.

The parents were worse than the kids. We were young lads who had come to play a game of football, and to listen to some of these people, you'd think we were there to burn their cars out. And once the kids heard Mammy and Daddy start with the usual stereotypical rubbish, they got that little bit braver and started mouthing off as well.

We would never let them see that it was hurting us. That was what they wanted. We swallowed whatever anger was there and played to shut people up with our football. As I got older, I found it more frustrating, because I was so proud to go out there and represent Ballymun, and yet these blinkered people still saw our heritage as some kind of hopeless disease that would suck all the good out of our lives. They didn't understand that our being from Ballymun wasn't something that we wanted to cure or shake or escape. It was everything to us.

We liked to think we were tough, and mentally, we had that bit of fight in us, but physically, we weren't the most intimidating. We were scrappy, maybe, but scrappiness was a survival instinct where we came from, and fighting was the only language that some lads knew. I was the kid that insisted on having the last word in a slagging match, but somehow, I managed to avoid getting into too many rows on the streets and in the school-yard. Most of the fights were little power plays that started over nothing and finished as quickly as they had started, but there was a lot of teenage energy that had to find an outlet somewhere, and if you were involved, you had no other option except to stand your ground. If you backed down, you might as well not show up.

We were actually quite small in size, and if you put us up alongside the kids from Ballyboden or St Brigid's, we looked a bit under-developed. These lads were playing rugby and basketball and all kinds of things from a young age and their physical profiles were really good. Brigid's had this monster playing in midfield, a big huge lad that they just kept kicking the ball to, and we couldn't get near him. He didn't even go on to play senior, as far as I know. Same with Boden, they had a basketball player who towered over everyone else and we just fouled him, every single time. What else could we do?

Sylvesters had a big lad too. In one of our games, he went up for a high ball against one of our players – no contest there – and the two of them ended up clattering into each other and going to ground. As they got back up, this giant took one look at our lad and clocked him. I was a few yards back from where it happened and I took off from a standing start. I launched myself straight at him, my whole body flying through the air like a wrestling move, and speared him. It was like chopping down a tree in slow motion. I hit him with some force, but it still took an eternity for him to come crashing down. It was around that time, while I was waiting for him to topple, that I realised how much trouble I was going to be in once he picked himself up. Thankfully a couple of lads had come flying in behind me as backup, and between us, we were able to get in just enough digs to settle the score.

I wish I could say that all of the fights I got into on the GAA pitch were like that, an instinctive reaction to protect myself and my teammates and make sure that we weren't being pushed around. That did happen quite a lot, but the truth is, I got into a lot of fights because I thought it was funny. It was that real attention-seeking kind of messing, where I thought it was great craic to have the other lads on the bus home going, 'Philly, you're mad,' or going back into school on Monday and telling the others, 'You'd want to see what Philly was at on Saturday.' I thought I was being hilarious and I definitely wasn't thinking about the impact that it might be having on the team.

It came to a head after a couple of weeks in a row where I was in fights in every match. Some of them I had been sent off; the others I'd managed to be smart enough to get away with a warning from the ref. Paddy pulled me to one side.

'I'm taking the captaincy off you,' he said. 'I'm sick of standing there watching you fighting all the time. We need a leader as our captain and you're obviously not able to do that, so we'll get someone else who can.'

His words knocked the wind out of me and I was immediately on the defensive, looking for somebody else to blame. How dare you, I thought, how dare you do that to me? I was so proud of being captain, and I had never even considered how disappointed I would be to lose it – which, of course, is precisely why Paddy did what he did. It was the only move he had left that would snap me out of that juvenile mindset, force me to take a step back and think.

It was a huge learning experience for me. I was far too used to seeing John and my friends get into trouble and then just laugh and shrug it off as if it didn't matter, and I had started to develop the same attitude myself. I couldn't go around behaving like my actions had no consequences, and then getting even more defiant when somebody pulled me up on it. That immaturity had cost me something that I cared about. I had to start taking responsibility. From that point on, there was no more fighting for fighting's sake, only when we needed it. The older I got, the more I came to appreciate that being there for your teammates didn't necessarily mean wading in swinging haymakers blindly. There were other ways to support each other and back each other up.

Sometimes, though, you just couldn't avoid it. Erin's Isle are one of our local rivals so it was never too surprising if there was a bit of an edge to the games. There had been a good bit of the usual scrapping, little things on and off the ball, and out of the corner of my eye I saw Davey go down holding his face. SMACK – this lad had just chinned Davey – and before I knew it, I was on top of him, punches raining in. I'm not sure if the ref sent me off or if I got away with it, if we won the game or lost. The only reason I remember that day is because of what happened next.

Davey is an angry man – we're always slagging him about his little man syndrome – and it was even worse when he was younger. The game was over and everything had settled down. There were no dressing rooms so ourselves and the Isles lads had been dispatched to our respective sidelines and we were all getting changed, but Davey was nowhere to be seen. Next thing, we heard this almighty crack coming from one of the big bushes in the corner of Albert College, a sound that could only be a branch snapping. I spun around and there he was, steam coming out of his ears, running for the Isles sideline swinging this stick that was twice the size of him.

'Davey, relax, you mad thing. It's grand.'

He was ready to sort your man out, not to mention anybody else that might have a notion to try to stop him. Thankfully, Hubby (Alan Hubbard) managed to grab a hold of him and calm him down before he did anything stupid.

Memories like that stick out for a few different reasons, but mainly because scraps were the exception rather than the rule. Put it this way: our team was involved in a lot more good football than we were in fights. Paddy just didn't allow them. The only time he wanted to see a closed fist was when we were handpassing the ball. He knew that if he condoned violence as part of our game, or if he allowed us to vent our frustration in that physical way, there was every chance that we'd change out of our GAA gear, go back home to our friends and families and classmates or whoever, and channel our energy in the same aggressive manner.

Part of it as well was that Paddy didn't want us feeding that stereotype that everyone from Ballymun was out of control. It's so easy for a young person's self-image to become wrapped up in that stigma and then it becomes self-perpetuating: I'm from Ballymun, and this is how outsiders see Ballymun, so this is how I have to behave. Paddy tried to drill discipline into us so we would see that we're the ones that choose who we want to be in life, nobody else.

For all of our talent, we didn't win anything coming up through the ranks at underage. We played some lovely football and we were hard to beat, especially at home in Poppintree Park and Albert College, but when it came to championship semi-finals or finals, from Féile all the way up, there were always one or two teams better than us.

Paddy wanted to coach a football team, not a fight club. All of the drills and skill sessions that he was putting us through meant that our technical ability was up there with anyone in the county. We had some great battles with Na Fianna, our local rivals from down the road, who had really talented players like Tomo Brady and Joey Boland coming through. Crokes had a very strong side as well. We were good enough to compete with, and beat, everyone – except for Brigid's.

Everybody knew what to expect when ourselves and Brigid's played each other. Word got around that these were two good young teams playing really nice football, and that you'd probably see a few future Dublin stars in the making. We obviously had a couple of lads, and then they had Paddy Andrews, who was head and shoulders above everybody else at that age, the kind of player who left you with no option but to double-mark him.

Albert College was absolutely rammed for the matches, crowds and crowds on the sidelines, going around the whole pitch. An unbelievable atmosphere as these games went one way, then the other, and then back again before Brigid's kicked a few points to pull clear of us, as they always did. It was a killer: we were so close to them and we just couldn't get over the line. I can't even imagine how many leagues and championships we could have won at underage if they hadn't been standing in our way.

That was Paddy's biggest challenge. He needed to keep us interested and keep us playing, and to do that, he needed us to believe that we could be better than second best.

---

Growing up, I was certainly protected, if not quite sheltered. But despite my parents' best efforts, the reality of life in Ballymun meant that nobody was ever really sheltered.

I have described my childhood memories of me and John as I experienced them at the time. The simple pleasures. The things that you cling onto and remember as you grow up and your eyes open to a much more complicated version of the world we live in.

I know now that they only tell a part of the story.

Because for nearly as long as I can remember, although I didn't realise it at the time, John was addicted to drugs.

Heroin destroyed my brother's life.

I often think about the decisions he made, the paths he walked, and why he walked them. I wonder how his life might have been different if he had been born seven years later, or how mine would have been if I was born seven years earlier and hit adolescence when he did, at the time when Dublin's drug problem had sunk its claws deepest into the city.

If he hadn't gone before me and made all of the mistakes that he made, would I have ended up using drugs? Probably. More so than any other influence in my life, his choices made me the person who I am today, and I will never forget that or take it for granted.

I chose sport. What did he choose? The truth is, he never had a choice. They were all taken away from him before he realised that his life could be anything that he wanted it to be, full of endless possibilities.

———

John didn't have much interest in sport. Anything he tried, he gave up just as quickly.

A few of his mates were good boxers, and John tagged along with them on the nights that they were going around to the club in St Pappin's. He'd throw on a pair of gloves and hit the bag or do a few rounds of sparring, but his heart was never really in it. He was far more interested in having the craic – too much craic for the coaches' liking anyway.

John tried pool, and for a while, he got really into it. He started for the same reasons as most of the rest of us, because he had nothing else to be doing and the pool hall was open and dry and warm, but he turned out to have a good eye for it. A local man, Martin Kirwan, was coaching the Irish team and he got John involved in one of their squads for travelling over to England and Scotland and Wales to play some other representative teams. I was on the Irish team myself for a while as a teenager, and played in some of those tournaments, but by that stage, John had given it up.

We were sitting at home one night when John bounced in the door, just back from a tournament in Wales. We never even got to ask if they'd won or lost. As soon as Mam saw John, standing there with his big goofy grin, her face dropped.

His neck looked something out of a Dracula film, teeth marks and all. His skin had obviously been chewed to bits at some point over the previous 48 hours and was now covered in more purple, red, yellow, and green than a bag of Skittles. You wouldn't even know if it was one vampire that had done the damage or an army of them. A necklace of lovebites.

'Get over to me,' Mam roared, grabbing him to get a closer look. 'What are you after doing to your neck?'

John didn't say much. What could he say? Knowing him, there wouldn't have been an ounce of romance in the whole escapade, it was all for show, to get a reaction from the lads. And through the look of pure disgust on Mam's face, wondering how she could have raised such a lunatic, you could definitely see the beginnings of a smile.

He tried Gaelic football as well, although I never knew that until a couple of years ago when I went back to Holy Spirit to give a talk. Those corridors were familiar enough to the two of us, I suppose, given that we both spent so much time over the years sitting outside in them rather than in the classroom. There are a couple of photos of me on the walls there now, celebrating after one of our All-Ireland wins, and when I stopped to have a look, one of the old photos of the school Gaelic football team caught the corner of my eye.

Mr Kelly, one of my old teachers, and Mr O'Connell, who ran the school team that I had played on, were showing me down to the hall where the talk was on.

'When's that from?' I pointed to the cheeky face in the back row, head and shoulders above his teammates. 'That's my brother John there.'

They hadn't a clue any more than I did. 'I didn't know he played football.'

'Neither did I,' I admitted, digging my phone out of my pocket to take a photo of the photo. It's there now every time I pick up my phone: John in his school GAA jersey as my screensaver.

Playing sport wasn't really John's thing, but he loved his gangsta rap and hip hop. He never picked a side between East

Coast and West, although Tupac would probably get the edge if you pushed him on it. There were always a couple of Biggie's CDS around the flat as well though, in there with the Wu Tang Clan, Dre, DMX, and Ja Rule. He tried to look the part too, packing out his wardrobe full of shiny tracksuits that he insisted on wearing at least three sizes too big and baseball caps that he pulled down until you couldn't see his eyes.

It wasn't Compton we were living in, although some lads probably wished it was. Whatever scraps were going on between our group in Sillogue and the others over in Shangan, or wherever the row was, it wasn't exactly the Bloods and the Crips. The nights I was allowed to hang around with John and his friends for a couple of hours, there could have been anywhere between 20 and 40 people, lads up to the usual shite as they tried to impress girls, smokes, cans, and 'Fuck Tha Police' on the radio, John at the centre of it telling jokes and stories while I knocked the ball around with Mick, or with Carl or Eamo, two of their other mates.

'Go on, Philly, give us a pass there,' as they handed off their joint for a second.

Apart from Mick, John never had any mates his own age. He was the baby of his group of friends, and the rest of them were all five or six years older, which made them 12 or 13 years older than me. In my eyes, they were the coolest lads in Ballymun – they just seemed to know so much about life and the world – and John worshipped them. He had no interest in making friends with anyone his own age, wasting time on an apprenticeship before graduating to hang out with the older group. He saw himself as way more streetwise and advanced than that. Other lads would run and get their da to solve their problems; John wanted to be around people who could look after themselves.

He never had a big brother and these lads were the next best thing. He looked up to them and they looked out for him. If there was any hassle, or John was in a fight, they were the ones that would hop in for him, his protection.

Or so he thought. The reality of it was that most of them were so tangled up in their own problems, they weren't really worried about John. They saw him as their little runner, someone who could stop them from getting their hands dirty when they didn't have to. They didn't see that they were drawing another teenager towards the same bad choices that they had made themselves. Or maybe they did, and they didn't care.

That was the price of admission and John bought a ticket. He obviously had that need to feel that he belonged. Maybe that's why he was such a messer and went out of his way to make people laugh. His first craving was for that validation and only the older lads could give it to him. But for all their talk, they wouldn't be there for him if the shit hit the fan. John had to find that out the hard way.

The lads are still down in the field. They've been there all day and now it's way past my bedtime, but they're not going anywhere.

There are vultures everywhere and all they see is prey. A man, a fully grown man well into his thirties, invites himself to join this party of teenagers. No, he doesn't want a swig of your cider or the end of your spliff, but here – do yis want a few pills, lads? Pass them around there. Go on, see yis later.

Bad enough that they're already a couple of litres of booze in. Ballymun is the country's biggest black-market pharmacy and you don't need a prescription to get your hands on the harder substances. The place is swarming with people who either don't know any better or don't care. It's the culture, the way things are, because it stands to benefit a handful of people and make them rich. It normalises the most crazy, irresponsible shit – adults giving kids pills without a second thought.

For John, it started with a bit of hash and a few hits of acid. When the lads you idolise are the ones holding out their hand and saying, 'Have half of this' or 'Try a bit of that,' you're not going to say no.

Drugs were a part of all of our worlds growing up in Ballymun, but for John they became a part of his day, a social ritual, and a currency. One of the lads presses a few grubby notes into the palm of his hand. 'Here, John, run around and get us a five spot there.'

John was always one to oblige, even when he wasn't trying to impress or fit in. If you asked him to go around to the van and get you a can of Coke, he wouldn't tell you to go and do it yourself like most other lippy young fellas might. He'd just go, and probably make sure that nobody else needed anything before he did.

He ducks off around the corner. He knows who to look for, and he knows what to get and how not to get ripped off. He comes back a minute or two later, hands over the little bag in his pocket, and then waits. Whoever was buying that night breaks a bit off the corner of the block of hash, enough for a couple of spliffs, and passes it to John. His delivery fee.

Before long, the jobs got bigger and bigger. Drug users in the late 1990s were drawn to Ballymun like it was a magnet. It was simple economics, supply and demand: they wanted gear, there were plenty of people there that were willing to sell it to them, and all of the trade concentrated in one area.

You always knew who was from the area and who wasn't, and you could spot these outsiders a mile away. When you play with fire, you get burned, and they were more vulnerable than they probably realised. They walked up to the lads on the blocks and flashed enough of a note to prove that they were good for it.

A nod or a whistle. 'See those two young fellas over there,' pointing towards John and Mick. 'They'll show you where to go.'

The two boys led the way into one of the blocks.

'Yeah, yeah, just up here,' as they ushered their wannabe customer up the stairs and into the darkness. The punch came from nowhere, their buyer blindsided and left in a heap, and whether or not he'd get his drugs quickly became the least of his worries. The two lads were standing over him, and they didn't look like young fellas any more.

'Give us your money now and we'll let you walk back down them stairs in one piece.' There wasn't much point in looking for help. Nobody would get involved and if anyone did answer the call, you could be sure they were coming to help John and Mick.

That was the business they were in, sent in by the older lads who were running the show to rip off drug users for their money.

And when you rip someone off like that, you can be sure they'll be back later and they won't be alone and they won't be looking for a friendly chat to see if they can have their money back and maybe pick up the drugs that they came looking for in the first place. When that car comes down the road and the window rolls down and someone shouts, 'That's the fucker there,' the older lads want to be sure that it's John or Mick that they're pointing at, not them.

One night, one of the lads set John and Derek up for a fight, stirring things between them until they were punching the head off each other and both doing damage. This was serious.

By the time it was all done, the two of them were in bits: black eyes, busted noses, lips swollen halfway up their face. And for what?

Next day, there was a knock on the door of the flat and John got up to answer it, his face still hopping with the swelling and bruises. Mick was standing there, and there was barely a word between them before they were wrapped in a bear hug and back to being best mates again.

Mick had told his dad the whole story that morning.

'What happened to you last night?'

'Nothing, Da. Was just an argument.'

'Who were you fighting?'

'It was nothing. Me and John just had a row about something.'

'Well, would you not go up to him and fucking sort it out now? Because if you don't do it today, you're not going to do it tomorrow.'

Mam had gone out and bought a PlayStation when nobody else we knew had one. It was her way of keeping John where she could see him. A lot of parents will nearly take the fuse out of the plug to force their kids to go outside and get some fresh air, but if he was in there playing video games, at least she knew where he was and he was safe. Mick sat down beside him, their faces in ribbons, and picked up a controller as if nothing had ever happened. They promised each other that nobody would ever set them up and turn them against each other like that again.

Back up on the block later on that day, they made that clear. If you ever do that again, the two of us will jump on you and kick the shite out of you.

———

You wouldn't spend any longer in the lifts than you had to. Unless you were hiding. Then they were as good a place as you'd find. There was a knack to getting them 'stuck' – leave the outer set of the double doors closed, force open the inner one, and then if anyone pushed the button to call it, it wouldn't move. You could be in there for hours, up to whatever.

A fist rattled off the steel. BANG BANG BANG. You wouldn't want to be jumpy or anything.

'Come out of there, yis little fuckers, or I'll bleedin' kill yous.'

The four lads crammed into the little box looked at each other. Whoever it was would give up eventually. They always did.

The oldest lad held out a small piece of tinfoil and a lighter. 'Do yis want a hit, lads, yeah?'

I don't care where you're from and what you've been exposed to. You're a little boy, barely a teenager, and someone puts heroin under your nose and you feel like their eyes are looking straight through you. It's a dare, it's a challenge, it's a test, and you don't know any better. How could you?

John fought against the confusion. Act like you know what's going on here. Be the big man.

'Yeah, what is it?' Mick was the one with the balls to say what they were all thinking.

'A bit of H, yeah,' he said, his arm still extended but his patience already wearing thin.

H? What's that?

Eamo reached across and took a hold of the straw. 'It's only liquid hash, lads, come on.'

And he did it. They all did. John was 14 when he took his first hit of heroin.

———

For all of his innocence and naivety, John was smart enough to cover his tracks with Mam and Dad. For the first couple of years anyway. If he came in late at night looking the worse for wear, he knew how far he could push it with them.

'I just had a bit of beer with the lads, Ma, I'm grand.' And inevitably he was. He'd bounce out of the bottom bunk right as rain the next morning and be ready to go.

My parents aren't stupid, and they weren't too pleased at the thought of their teenage son out skulling cans until all hours, but in the grand scheme of things, they knew that there was worse mischief that a lad of his age could be getting up to.

John left school when he was 16, but, to be honest, the writing was on the wall from the age of about six or seven. Mam got a call from the office in Holy Spirit, the primary school around the corner that we all went to. Would she mind coming down? There was something that they needed to speak to her about. I'd say Mam quickly lost track of the amount of times that she made that walk over the years, first to Holy Spirit and then later to the Comp. There was always something going on, and it was rarely good.

Walking in the door, she could feel the giddiness in the air, and inside the classrooms the sound of frustrated teachers trying to rein in the excess energy and restore some order. And there was John, sitting up outside the office like butter wouldn't melt, but that glint of mischief still in his eye after setting off the fire alarm.

When I was young, I couldn't understand why he wasn't afraid of getting in trouble in school. 'Ah sure, look,' he told me, 'I just sit down in the principal's office and it goes in one ear and out the other.' While I let that little misguided life lesson sink in, Dad sat across the room glaring at John with a face that said you'll get a clip around the ear if you keep thinking that way.

I had a pretty good idea of how often he was in trouble because every time Mam got called up to the office, I was dragged along too. One day as we were leaving the office, Mr Manning, the vice-principal in Holy Spirit, handed me a pound coin. 'Don't be a messer in school,' he said to me. That stuck with me as well, although if I had taken his words on board a bit more, I probably wouldn't have spent as much time sitting outside the classroom myself.

Nothing much changed when John moved on to secondary school, and sitting the Leaving Cert was never on his agenda. Mam, her heart broken by the whole thing, was over and back to the Comp for meetings with the principal, Frank Byrne, as the two of them tried to figure out what to do with him. When John left school, Mr Byrne helped him to get onto a course in a place called Ballark, a local community training scheme, and then he got his first real job in the Meat Packers. He'd come back home in the evenings stinking of meat and blood, and the smell would take over the flat. It would nearly put you off your dinner, absolutely rotten.

'Fuck's sake. The guards are at me again, Ma, they won't leave me alone.' We got used to hearing the same conversation over and again when John came in from work.

'What did they want this time?'

'Same thing. Strip search. They keep searching me for drugs.'

It was always the same guard, and it always seemed to be John that she was picking up. We presumed it was because he had that drawn, lanky look about him – but that was just John. Mam was furious. She was over and back to the Garda station to file complaints and harassment reports on his behalf. Of course the guards probably knew something that we didn't.

John wasn't making a huge amount of money, but he was still at home, and it should have been comfortably enough for the life that we thought he was living. A bit of rent money for Mam to help pay for the shopping and the bills, and a few quid then to see him through the rest of the week. It was only when he got hurt that my parents started to realise that something was up.

He came in, his arm wrapped in a massive bandage. Mam nearly lost it with the fright when she saw him.

'Jesus, John, what happened to you?'

He sat down at the table and told them the story. There had been an accident on the factory floor that afternoon. He was working away and whatever machine he was using had gone dodgy, and it sliced his arm open.

'We're going to have to go to court,' Mam warned him. 'Whatever you do, John, you're not to take any money that they offer you before that, right? Do you hear me?'

Mam was right. His arm was OK, or at least it would be in a week or two, but the compensation claim was still worth a lot, probably about £8,000 for an injury like that. If the factory thought they were on the hook for a pay-out, it wouldn't be long before their lawyers were involved and starting to push for a settlement.

A couple of weeks went by, and then a couple more. John was back at work, but Mam had heard nothing from him about the claim or a court date. It was as if the accident had never happened, and John had gone fairly quiet. He wasn't at home as much, spending more time with Mick, and with the girl that he was seeing at the time.

Mam got a hold of him eventually.

'John, what's going on with your claim? Have you heard anything?'

'No, Ma, nothing.'

First he told her that he had never got anything, and then he came clean with the truth.

'They paid me a bit. I took it.'

The one thing that Mam had warned him not to do. It was only a fraction of what John really should have been entitled to. She was fit to kill him.

Dad was as confused as Mam was.

'Why did you take the money? You would have got more from them in court.'

'I just needed the money so I took it.'

'Where is it? Where did you put it?'

The way John was shifting from one foot to another, like he was ready to leg it out the door, they knew it wasn't good news.

'It's gone.'

———

The rows seemed like they would go on for days at a time. Mam would grab him, Dad would grab him, as if literally shaking sense into him was the only thing that might work.

'Stop lying to us, John. We know you're on drugs.'

They didn't know how to talk to him, and he didn't know how to talk to them, and all of the worry and fear and guilt and shame just came out as screams and shouts until John stormed out only to come back a few hours, or a few days, later. There were nights when Mam cried herself to sleep, and her only dream was that she would wake up the next morning and that John would have changed.

Reasoning with him didn't work, and neither did begging him. Having a heroin addict as a son and a brother was a dirty secret, and once we discovered it, it felt like every door slammed shut in our faces. We couldn't see anybody who could help us. Who could we talk to, when nobody would understand? Even in a community that had gone through the same experience hundreds of times, we felt isolated and alone.

How else do you come to a stage where you feel that the only thing you can do is to put your 17-year-old son out on the street? To turn your back on him and lock the door at night?

How does something so extreme become the only viable option? As John fell deeper and deeper into his addiction, he pushed Mam to breaking point, and this was the only way through the darkness that she could see.

She opened the drawer where she kept her rings and her heart sank immediately. She didn't even need to check any of the other places where she kept her jewellery. She knew she wouldn't find it. It was gone.

Every ring, every bracelet and necklace, every set of earrings that was in the house. All gone.

We knew things were bad, that he was struggling, but at that point I don't think any of us realised how low John would go to get his fix.

Mam got a hold of him. More tears and more screaming and more shouting, and part of her wanted to know what he had done with all of her stuff and part of her just wanted her little boy back.

She grabbed her keys from the hall and went out. She didn't need John to tell her which doors to go knocking on. She went from dealer to dealer, explaining who she was and what she wanted. Pleading with them, her purse in her hand. Here, take the money, could she just have her jewellery back. She'd pay them whatever.

And when she came home, wrecked and empty-handed, she knew that she couldn't take any more.

John wasn't blind. He could see the hurt he was causing to all of us, but especially to his ma, the one person that he loved more than anyone in the world. That's why people think that tough love works, that if you hold the most important personal relationship in an addict's life to ransom, it will be the trump card that finally forces them to change their ways. But it doesn't always work like that.

You can't comprehend how that little piece of chalk, that bit of powder, can be more powerful than love. Much more powerful than love. You don't want to believe it, but that's the reality.

———

Mam looked out the window and spotted him. Back on the blocks, surrounded by a huge gang, guys and girls, standing right in the middle of them all.

It had been a while since she had put him out of the house and none of us knew where he had been. If John didn't want to be found, he wouldn't be found, that's for sure. It killed Mam to put him out in the first place, and now that she couldn't keep an eye on him for herself, all sorts of worst-case scenarios filled the space where he should have been. Every knock on the front door brought fresh anxiety. Mam would get up in the morning and go off to work and you'd know she'd barely slept a wink. She'd never let it show though. In a lot of respects, she was the strongest of us all.

She'd had enough though.

'Phil,' she called my dad, 'go over there and get him back in here now, will you?'

Dad is a big man – he looks like Walter White from *Breaking Bad* these days, with the bald head and the beard – and he was trying to stay out of sight as he got closer and closer to where they were standing, watching them to see what was going on. He must have lost patience because suddenly he just marched straight over, pushed his way into the middle of the circle, and grabbed a hold of John by the collar.

'What the fuck?'

It happened so quickly that John didn't know what was going on. Neither did any of the others. They were all ready for a fight.

'The fuck? Kill your man.'

John wriggled around enough, saw a face that wasn't messing, and called them off.

'Fuck off, would yis – it's grand, it's my da.'

There was no arguing. Dad marched him back across the road, into the flat, and put him into the bath. The next morning, Mam had a brand new tracksuit laid out for him by the time he got out of bed. He was right as rain.

In those initial years, John was using heroin on a regular basis, but at a level that meant he was still able to get up in the morning and go to work. After he lost his job at the Meat Packers, Mam and Dad did everything they could to find him jobs and keep him in some sort of a daily routine, working on construction sites with Dad first and then later with the security company that Mam looked after.

When he had a bit of money in his pocket, he wasn't in a position where he had to steal to feed his addiction, and the day that he sold off Mam's jewellery was an exception really at that time. The one time he robbed money from me, he made sure that he paid me back every last penny.

I was good with money from a young age. Dad was a great man for encouraging us to save, and there was always a few quid on offer at the end of the week provided my room was clean or the hoovering around the flat was done. It all went into a little money tin in my room. I could feel it getting more and more full with every fiver, and I couldn't wait to get it open and count it all up and start thinking about what to buy. When I finally took the lid off it, all of the coins were still there, but there wasn't a single note left in it. John had taken them all.

We eventually found out how he had done it. I had noticed that the slit at the top of the tin was getting wider and wider, and there were little scrapes on the inside of the opening. When he'd paid me back in full – about £80 I think, which was a lot for me at the time – I asked him how he'd managed to get the money out without breaking open the tin. He took a hairpin out of his pocket – he'd been fishing the notes off the top one at a time.

After the jewellery, Mam and Dad watched him like a hawk. One night, they were in watching TV and he tried to sneak in past them. When they heard the door close, quietly, they knew something was up.

'Come here, you,' Dad called him, and there was no point in John pretending that he hadn't heard him. 'Come here. Put your hands up.' That was an order.

It was as if the Gardaí themselves had walked in the door and picked John up to do a random search. Dad started to pat him down, and next thing, he put his hand into John's pocket and found a little brown block, like a tiny corner of a cube of Bisto, barely bigger than a pinhead.

He held it up in front of him. 'What's this?'

'It's letting-on heroin, Da – it's not real or anything,' John said, not taking his eyes off Dad's hand for a second.

'Letting-on heroin? Come on with me so,' Dad said, and went into the bathroom and flushed it down the toilet.

John stood there and watched him, his fix for the next day gone.

As I got a little bit older, I had a better understanding of what was going on in his life. I'd see bits of foil that had fallen out of his jacket pocket or that he'd left lying around our bedroom, and I'd know what they meant. I was afraid to even touch them. He hid his drug use and he wouldn't have done it in the house, but he got to a stage where the drug had taken over so completely that he didn't even think about what he looked like or if other people noticed him taking it. When you're at that point, the addiction is in control; nothing else matters.

John never took drugs around me, though, at any stage. In one way, that was the only thing we could do to keep an eye on him. For a while, Mam tried to insist that he take me with him if he was going out at night.

'Do not let him out of your sight tonight,' she'd tell me, and I'd stick to John like glue. Just a few years earlier he had been the one babysitting me, and now it felt like the roles had been reversed. It worked though, for a night or two at least.

When you spend a lot of time around a drug addict, it's very easy to tell the difference between the times when they are using heroin and the times when they are using methadone. Most of the time, you can tell just by looking at them.

John always had that real skinny frame, but as the heroin took its toll, he looked more and more drawn. The poison was coming out through the sores in his face, the heroin, whatever chemicals it had been cut with, the toxic fumes from the burnt tin foil. Deep down, he was still John but he looked nothing like the brother I remembered.

When he tried to come off heroin and started to take methadone, he ballooned out, 10 times the size. His face was huge and his fingers were like sausages because of all the water that his body was retaining. He didn't look any healthier.

Methadone didn't help John. In fact, it probably made him worse.

He got so bad and Mam got so worried that she begged him to go up with her and see someone in the Redbrick – Domville House is its real name – which was the only sort of treatment service available in the area. There were some great staff up there, who worked day and night to try to help, but it was a horrible, hopeless place. They had their way of doing things, their set treatment plans and programmes, and it was their way or the highway. Mam sat beside John, trying to take in all this information that they were being bombarded with, before the two of them were rushed back out the door again with a few leaflets and a methadone script. Their services were under so much pressure, hundreds of people in treatment at this one clinic, and they didn't want to explain, they didn't want to discuss. They couldn't.

The logic behind methadone treatment is that it is a weaker drug and so it helps to transition addicts away from heroin, and then the dosage can gradually be made smaller and smaller until the person is completely clean of all drugs.

The reality of it was that the government were forcing people onto methadone so that they could point to the number of heroin addicts getting lower and lower and say that they were tackling the problem. It was one less heroin addict, sure, but they were creating a new methadone addict, and because the methadone hit is weaker, a lot of addicts start taking other drugs to try match the buzz that they used to get.

The Redbrick became a focal point for dealers. It made their job even easier for them. All they had to do was stand outside the front door and pick off the recovering addicts one by one as they walked out. Driving down the Ballymun Road, it was the same story every time – dozens of bloated addicts, and somewhere in the midst of them, one skinny fella with the flashy tracksuit and whatever drugs they needed.

At best, the government's methadone push just moved numbers from one column to another; they didn't seem to realise that every single one of those numbers was a life like my brother's. We weren't equipped to handle having a heroin addict in our family, and the governments of the 1990s and early 2000s certainly weren't equipped to handle having thousands of them in the country.

Some people did successfully come through treatment and get clean, but so many more were caught in a trap like John. The doses that doctors were prescribing him kept getting higher and higher until John was at a level on methadone that he was never used to on heroin.

There was murder when Mam went up to the Redbrick. She couldn't understand it.

'Why are you giving him so much phy?' she asked – physeptone, the brand name for methadone.

They explained that they needed to stabilise John first before bringing him off it, but they never brought him off it. Maybe he wasn't ready to come off.

John went into town and jumped on the DART, doing his best not to notice the eyes that were staring at him, hoping that he wouldn't pick the free seat beside them. It became part of his weekly routine, that trip out to Bray to the doctor who would fill his methadone prescription for him. An hour later, he was back on the train again with a little bottle in his pocket: 200mls of green, a full week's supply of the medication in one go.

———

John's addiction changed him in a lot of ways, but it could never kill his kind heart. The neighbours knew him, but as he sank deeper and deeper into trouble, most of them kept their distance. His first instinct was always to help, even if it meant putting himself in harm's way.

He went out to do a bit of construction work with Dad on a project that they had out in Inchicore. The two of them were up on the roof of the building, just finished up for the day, and Dad started to climb down. Halfway down, the ladder gave way on him and Dad started falling backwards. All John heard was a roar and then the thump of Dad's body hitting the ground.

Before Dad even had a chance to pick himself up off the tarp and make sure that nothing was broken, John came flying off the roof after him like Geronimo.

'DA, DA! Are you alright?'

Dad got up and gave him a clatter. 'You fucking eejit.'

Dad had fallen onto a second smaller roof, so the damage wasn't too serious, but John didn't even think before he jumped after him. On the other side of the roof, there was a 60-foot drop, all sorts of machinery, and if John had fallen there, he would have been killed.

'Did you know this was here?' Dad asked him.

John hadn't a clue.

'Then what are you doing jumping off a roof after me?!'

That was just John's way. There's a neighbour in Ballymun who still remembers what he did for her when he was in the pits of his addiction and has never forgotten him for it. John was on the blocks, and in a bad state, when this woman dropped everything she had on the side of the road. Purse, bags of shopping, the lot. And as she scrambled to get her things together, John came over to gather up her stuff and bring it back to the flat for her. It would have been the easiest thing in the world for him to see an opportunity there and take advantage, for her purse or her car keys to go missing. If you listen to the way a lot of people stereotype addicts, that's what they would expect.

All he wanted to do was help, but I couldn't see that. I couldn't see that underneath it all he was still John, the big brother I adored. I couldn't see past the addiction. I was so embarrassed by him that I changed my name.

My mam and dad aren't married. Mam is a Caffrey, and we were all raised as Caffreys, but I was so ashamed of John, so ashamed to have a heroin addict in my family, as my brother, that I changed my name to McMahon, Dad's surname. I had been so proud to be Young Caffo growing up. Now I wanted to put as much distance between us as possible.

I got into an argument in the pool hall one night. Myself and this other lad were mouthing off at each other, the usual nonsense, and an older guy butted in. I was only a kid at the time, still at the stage where I'd threaten to get John if anyone came near me.

'Go on and get your brother,' the older lad sneered at me. 'He's only a junkie.'

Everyone in the place started laughing and I was so hurt. Really, I was more furious at John because it was true, because he had put me in that position, than I was at your man for saying it.

People in Ballymun might have been able to relate to what we were going through, but the further out of that circle I went, the more embarrassed I got. I was starting to get called into Dublin development squads, mixing with teenagers from all different parts of the city, and I was so aware that none of them had brothers who were addicted to heroin. It was eating me up. If they ever found out, I would have been humiliated.

'Here, are you Pillar Caffrey's son?' lads asked me.

'No no no,' I explained. 'My name is actually Philly McMahon. It's only Caffrey by law.'

Over the years, it was very hard for me when the families came back to hotels after matches, or if we went on a team night out together.

'Philly, come here, I want you to meet my brother. This is …'

And you'd shake hands and have the craic, and in the back of your head you'd always be thinking, why is my brother not like that? Why can't I do things like this with my brother?

All I wanted was to have a normal family. I thought everybody else had perfect lives, that nobody else had their own problems to be dealing with, that we were the only ones, and it made me so angry at John. I'd see him hanging around the blocks and I'd know what he was at, and I'd just walk right past him or turn and go the other way – my own brother. I couldn't bear to look at him, couldn't bear to talk to him, couldn't even bear to acknowledge his existence at times. I didn't want anybody to know that we were related. I wanted nothing to do with him.

I couldn't talk to him about what he was going through. Instead I kept pushing him away. We were sitting around the table for dinner and John started up again.

'Wait till I tell yis this one,' he said, his usual laughing and messing, and I immediately tuned out, pushed the food around my plate with my fork, and concentrated on the peas and potatoes in front of me instead.

What is there to laugh about, John? I thought to myself. You're a heroin addict. Nothing about our lives is funny any more.

I was so fixated on John's addiction that I forgot about him, the person, my brother. I didn't care what he wanted to say or why he wanted to say it; I just wanted him off drugs. I couldn't see that he was trying to hide his problems with happiness, that he had so much negativity in his life that he wanted to try to bring some positivity to a family dinner, to give himself and all of us a break.

Instead I was locked in to my anger and frustration, and my reaction only made things worse. He knew I wasn't listening to him. He must have. I wanted him to get better, but ignoring him only put more distance between the two of us, made him feel more disconnected and isolated. It was a mistake.

Whether it was heroin or methadone, John couldn't break free. When Mam and Dad felt that they had to put him out again, he went onto the homeless list. He eventually found a place to stay in a halfway house out in Swords, and then in one in Dorset Street. Mam and Dad did everything they could to help him, renting him an apartment on Clonliffe Road, then one in Phibsborough.

Nothing worked. No matter where he was living, John could not disconnect from other addicts and his addiction. He came back in from Swords on the bus to get his dole, and all of the same fellas that he'd known through the years were still hanging around on the blocks. When he was living in shelters and halfway houses, he was with addicts every day. Even when he had his own place, or later when he was living in London, he kept falling in with the same type of people, in the same type of trouble.

It was no coincidence. Treatment services and counselling have got better and better over the years, but they cannot defeat the power of the stigma that society attaches to drug addiction. That's the real danger. Once you've made that mistake – and everybody makes mistakes – it isolates you.

John couldn't break that cycle because he felt that he belonged when he was around them. Being with other addicts was all that he knew.

———

From a distance, you wouldn't have noticed anything out of the ordinary. We were hanging around kicking a ball off the block. Absolutely unremarkable in every sense, except for the conversation that we were having.

We weren't big on the deep and meaningful chats, but for some reason that day, we were talking about life – hopes, dreams, ambitions, fears, that sort of thing. Myself and Steo were on the fringes of the conversation, more interested in the little game we had going between ourselves than anything else that was being discussed.

'Philly?'

'What?'

'What are you going to do?'

'What?'

The circle had worked its way around to me. By the time I was 17 or 18, at least I had some plan in mind, no matter how half-baked it was.

'Eh … I'm going to go on to college.'

I didn't even say university. University would have been another step again, another huge leap between what was possible and what was plausible. Going to college, any college, was ambitious enough for starters.

I might as well have said that I was going to invent time travel. There were a couple of seconds where the words just hung in the air, the lads waiting to see if I was going to elaborate any further on this craziness or, more likely, waiting for me to go, 'Aaaaaah no, I'm only messing.' Good one, Philly.

One of the lads piped up.

'Yeah yeah, you can't go to college,' he said. 'College is for poshies.'

He was right, wasn't he? People from Ballymun didn't go to college. College was for poshies. At least, that was the message we had been fed so often that we had no other choice but to begin to believe it, and that was exactly why I wanted to go and do it. I didn't do it to prove a point to my friends or family or anyone else in the world. I did it because I knew they were wrong. I could do it.

I look back now and I'm so proud of the choices I made, and of what I achieved. Nobody can ever take that away from me and they have made me who I am today. But for every story like mine, there are far too many that don't have such a happy ending.

Flip that situation around on its head. There's a young lad from Ballymun, a really lovely fella from a great family, a brilliant hurler with Setanta, and he's a part of this group of mates having a chat while me and Steo kick the ball off the wall.

'What are you going to do?' I ask him.

'Dunno.'

'What about college?' I ask.

And he laughs it off as some sort of impossible dream, because that's not how the world works when you're from Ballymun and society has conditioned us to accept this myth of hopelessness. Just as I'm making my choices, he's making his, with one massive difference. He hasn't had that role model in his life who has gone and made all those mistakes for him, like I have with John. When a lot of my friends started to experiment, John never let me touch drugs, never even let me consider it.

And so this particular lad starts using drugs, and he meets a girl who is also using drugs, and they start going out, and then the two of them need money so he starts selling drugs. And then the dealer who is selling him the drugs gets pissed off about something or other and threatens his life. And he is terrified, so he kills the dealer out of fear. He is in prison now for murder.

I know how grateful I should be. I'm grateful for the people who shaped me into who I am and for the opportunities that came my way. I had sport, I had John and I had a chip on my shoulder that never allowed me to settle for what other people expected of me.

———

I was born on 5 September 1987. Anybody who has played sport in Ireland will tell you that it's much better to be a January baby than a December baby. If the cut-off date to be eligible for a certain age grade is on 1 January, all of those kids born in January have nearly have a full year's growth advantage over the kids that are born in December.

September isn't quite as bad, but it still falls towards the wrong end of the calendar. The same thing happened when I first started school. Because I was born in September, my first day in junior infants was a few days before my fourth birthday and I was a lot younger than practically everybody else. Every year, I felt the other students were that bit more mature and better able to concentrate whereas I had no attention span at all. Being academic wasn't for me. It was much easier to be the class clown.

Exams and degrees were never the focus in our house. When my parents were growing up, society was pushing young people out into the workplace, and Mam and Dad never went to college or to university, although my eldest sister June did a bit of studying and Kellie, who is only a couple of years older than me, is an accountant and had to sit all of the professional exams to get her qualifications.

I was poor in school for lots of reasons. My attention span was non-existent, although I didn't have ADHD or anything like that. Again, I thought it was funny to be the messer and the one who was making everybody laugh. Being intelligent definitely wasn't cool either. When I go into schools to give talks now, I always say that one of the regrets I have is that I didn't hang around with lads who took their education a bit more seriously – or even just lads who did their homework – and it's true. Maybe some of their positive influence would have rubbed off on me.

Above all, once I started to struggle academically, I tried to hide it by messing. It's like everything: if I'm sitting down and

I'm not interested in what I'm doing, I'm going to do something else. Plus if I was outside the door rather than in the classroom, nobody could ask me a question that I wouldn't know the answer to and embarrass me.

I can see now as well that part of the problem is with the curriculum that is taught in Irish schools. Children aren't encouraged to be expressive and creative and, instead, it's drummed into you that you need to be able to remember all of these facts and then just reproduce them in an exam. The Leaving Cert is a pure memory test. That didn't help me at all because I was much more suited to the creative subjects. Dad was always good at art, had a great eye for a drawing, and at one stage, I even thought about going to art college.

Outside of the art room I was a handful, but there were a lot of good, young teachers in the Comp who were able to relate to us. Unfortunately, no matter how great they were and no matter how much they tried to get through to me, I wasn't bothered making any sort of effort for the Leaving Cert. I had no ambitions to fill out a CAO form or go on to third-level education, so what use was a good Leaving Cert to me? I don't even know if I counted my points when I got my results, 200 or 250, some number which wasn't going to open too many doors for me.

I was 17 leaving school and my future stretched out in front of me like a long, open road with no signposts. In Ballymun, if you hung on in school until 17 or 18 and got through the Leaving Cert, that was a success in itself. But when I went up to training with Kickhams, the lads from Glasnevin on the team – Hubby, Trigger (Elliott Reilly), Eoin Dolan, Michael Lowther, Collie Moore – they were having a very different conversation.

'You doing honours or pass in that?'

'How many points?'

'That in DCU or UCD?'

It was like a different world. These lads had been brought up to see the Leaving Cert as the beginning, not as the end, a stepping stone that would help them to chase whatever career they were hoping for.

That's not to say that every lad I know from the other side of the wall went on to study in university – there were plenty who left school and dived straight into work – but in general they had ambition and a plan and they were applying themselves and fighting hard to get it. They weren't afraid of putting themselves out there or worried about what people might think if they fell short. Spending time around them changed how I saw myself and my future. I wanted what they had.

Playing football gave me confidence. It gave me purpose. It drew me into a world that was more than just rudderless boredom and mischief for mischief's sake. I was getting called into Dublin development squads, and then later onto the county minor panel, and I was surrounded by people who wanted to help me to be the best I could be, coaches and physios and nutritionists. They were invested in me. They cared about me.

That blue jersey became my mission. I wanted to wear it, to play in it, and I wanted people to see me in it and know. Anybody couldn't just wake up in the morning and decide to be a Dublin footballer. Famous people were Dublin footballers. Paddy Christie was a Dublin footballer. You have to have something special. I could be special. As my brother and my friends lost themselves further and further down one path in life, I found what I was looking for in the opposite direction.

Ambition started to creep into other parts of my life. When I left school, I knew that I needed to either get a job or sign up for a course somewhere. I was practical about it. Sport was what I was good at, and there was a two-year certificate in sport and leisure management on offer in Coláiste Íde. That didn't seem like it was going to be boring or too much like hard work, and it was handy because it was only down the road in Finglas. I enrolled and went home and told my parents that I was going to college.

A lot of people see PLC courses, like that one in Coláiste Íde, as a bridge between the Leaving Cert and going on to study for a degree or a higher-level qualification. I'd be lying if I said that that was my plan at the time, but it turned out to be the best decision I ever made. Doc and Cathal, two of my good friends from home, both started at the same time as well, and I met some more really sound lads there: Michael Doyle, Darragh Hanniffy, Sam, Philly, and Rory O'Connor, who was a very funny man long before he ever started the brilliant 'Rory's Stories' sketches.

We were sitting in class in one of our first weeks there, and the teacher went around the room.

'Tell us your name, a little bit about yourself, and what you're hoping to do when you've qualified from the course.'

The course was very heavy on sports and exercise and fitness modules, so a lot of people were hoping to use it as a first step into PE teaching. When it came to me, I said that I wanted to do teaching too.

I said that, but I didn't really believe it. I wasn't thinking that far ahead. One person said they wanted to start their own gym. The prospect couldn't have been further from my mind. I was sitting there listening and I thought, you'd want to be minted to open a gym, you must be crazy. At the time, nobody in Ireland was opening gyms, nobody was even thinking about it, but, as it happened, from that group of about 20, five or six ended up starting gym businesses – myself included.

It was in Coláiste Íde that I met Myra. Myra was the instructor for the swimming modules of our course and, like all of those great teachers that I had in the Comp, she had that empathy and understanding and you knew that she just got what you were about. I was out of school and I was supposed to be standing on my own two feet financially, but I was broke. I didn't want to be going to my parents every week with my hand out, even though there was never any question that they would support me in whatever I needed. I wanted to show that I was growing up and a bit more independent than that.

Myra came to me one day with a suggestion.

'Philly, are you still looking for a job?'

She had my attention immediately.

'There's a sign up in the club looking for a lifeguard. I can put you in touch with them if you're interested?'

The club was the Arena Health and Fitness Club out in Malahide. Myra seemed pretty confident that I would be well able for it, and she'd be happy to recommend me. Was I interested? I was a 17-year-old looking for whatever bit of money I could get my hands on – of course I was interested. I had been helping Mam a bit, doing bits of part-time work for one of her security companies, but this was a chance to have an actual job as well as keeping up the course, and it wouldn't really interfere with my football either, which was the priority. It sounded perfect.

It didn't take long for reality to kick in. I barely had my eyes closed when the alarm went off again the next morning like a siren in my ear. Half-awake and barely more than half-dressed, I rolled down to Coláiste Íde for a day of fitness classes and swimming and everything else that the course entailed, and then in the afternoon, hopped into my little Mitsubishi Colt with its tinted windows and massive exhaust and drove to Malahide for work. A couple of evenings a week, I'd have training with the Dublin minors on top of that as well, and when you added it all up, it just wasn't sustainable, even for a teenager with infinite amounts of energy. I was already wrecked by the time I got to Malahide, and then I was sitting in a chair in this roasting hot swimming pool and I was nodding off. I was piling training sessions on my body in that fatigued state and wondering why I was feeling flat. More than once on the drive back home at night, I clipped a kerb, purely down to lack of concentration. It was dangerous.

I knew I had to find something closer to home before I did damage to myself or to someone else. I rang Marc Hartigan, who had been over at Forest on trial with me that time. He was working as a duty manager in a big gym that was much closer to home. Any chance he could swing a job for me?

Marc's a great lad, and whatever good word he put in on my behalf, it worked. I loved that job initially, but I very quickly realised that that gym was everything that the fitness industry shouldn't be. All of the good practices that I was learning on my course, it was the exact opposite in this place.

It was like Globo Gym in the film *Zoolander*, all about getting people through the door, getting their cash into your hand, and getting them back out again so that you could get the next lot in. You weren't even giving your clients any specialised training when they were with you. You'd have a generic programme ready to go, stick one person on a treadmill, stick the next person on a cross-trainer, and bounce from one to the next with about eight different clients on the go at the same time.

I hated it, even though I was working with Marc who was a great mate, and I met and made friends with some other amazing people who I'm still in contact with today. It was sucking away at whatever passion I had for the industry. Don't get me wrong, we still had our craic, like the wrestling matches we had in the big open reception area when everything was locked up and everyone else was gone home. Working there was the best and worst thing that ever happened to me, because years later when it came to setting up my own gym and developing its systems and culture, I already knew everything that I didn't want it to be.

Eventually it came to a head – not because I was disillusioned, but because the gym's manager effectively forced me to choose between my job and my football. I was in my first year with the Dublin U21s at that stage and when I asked about the possibility of switching to morning shifts so that I could keep my evenings free for training, I was told there was no flexibility. That was that decision made. I wasn't exactly sorry to be going.

———

I always wanted the nice car, the kind that we would have been fighting to get into when Paddy was giving lifts up to training or a match. I knew exactly what I wanted too. I found a beautiful Audi A4 up the North, traded in the Mitsubishi Colt for it, and brought it back over the border. I spent more money looking after it than I would have on a child, and if there was a way to soup it up and spec it out, I had it – the S4 body kit, the 20-inch alloys, the whole lot.

I was young and a little naive, and once I had a relatively steady income of my own, I started eyeing up ways to spend it. I felt like I was running myself ragged between work, college, and football, and I wanted something to show for it, something to prove that all the sacrifices were worth it. I couldn't afford €13,000 for the Audi, of course, but I didn't mind getting a car loan to cover it. Taking on that debt and meeting monthly repayments wasn't really a major problem in my head as long as I had a job. Which I didn't now. So it became a problem.

I called the same person that I usually called whenever I ran into an issue like that.

'Paddy, you don't know of any jobs going anywhere, do you?'

Paddy had studied in DCU before going on to do his teacher training in St Pat's, and he had kept up those connections in the university. A couple of quick favours later, I was in touch with all the right people and I had a job working in the DCU gym.

It wasn't like he waved a wand and found me a job that magically made everything better. It was still as tough as ever to balance all of my different commitments and make sure that they were all getting the time and energy that they needed. Working in DCU gave me a new lease of life though. For starters, hundreds of inter-county footballers have passed through there over the years, and while there were still days when I felt like I was stretched beyond breaking point, the people I was working with there had seen it all before. They understood the pressure I was under and they made it their business to accommodate me.

More than that, it opened my eyes to a different side of the fitness industry, the exact opposite to the nightmare Globo Gym. I made friends like Martina McCarthy, who had run for Ireland at the Olympics in Sydney and was the DCU high performance manager, and lads like Robbie Bourke, Stephen Bennett and Graham Byrne who were working in strength and conditioning. These were all experts at the top of their game, and they were surrounding themselves every day with a mixture of established athletes and the stars of tomorrow in one of the best training facilities in the country. Everything was geared towards training the best to make them even better. It was a whole new world that I had never seen before, but I knew right away that I would like it.

DCU should have been an intimidating, daunting place full of unfamiliar faces who were bound to be more accomplished than me and my 200-odd Leaving Cert points, and it obviously was a little bit, but I never had that niggly fear that I was out of my depth or seconds away from being found out as a spoofer. It helped that I was there initially as a trainer and not as a student, and when it came to exercise and physiology, I was confident that I could hold my own. I had been in elite performance environments with the Dublin minors and U21s, and straight away, I felt like I understood, I belonged, and I could contribute.

I might have thought that I knew it all when I started, but I quickly realised that I had so much more to learn. I began to appreciate the depth of sports science as a vast field of knowledge and research and, for one of the first times in my life, I was passionate about the subject and I wanted to learn.

Martina would stop me – 'Why did you do it that way?' – and 15 minutes later we'd still be discussing different approaches or theories that might be better or worse. For the first time in my life, I was sneaking into lectures as opposed to sneaking out of classes in school. I wanted to take the words that I was reading in books and magazines and on the internet and put them into action in my work in the gym. I was hooked on that routine of learning and improving and learning again and improving again.

At the back of my head, that little voice of doubt was still there, faint enough that I could block it out most of the time but persistent enough that I could never fully forget about it. None of my friends had been to university, none of my family had been to university. College is for poshies. You shouldn't be here.

But every single day I was surrounded by students and working with them and I could see that we all had two eyes, two ears, a nose, a mouth, and some degree of a brain behind it all, so we weren't that different. And the Glasnevin lads down in Kickhams – why would something like this be within their reach, but out of mine? The more I was exposed to the university environment and the people in it, the more I realised that this was something I could chase for myself if I really wanted it.

When you don't believe in yourself, it's easy to focus on the obstacles and talk yourself down before you ever take that leap of faith. If I wanted to, I could have found plenty of 'good reasons' – excuses – not to even bother with college. Instead of settling back into the safe, comfortable bubble that you create for yourself when your ambitions are limited, I went looking for some positive affirmation that would build up my self-belief, not undermine it.

I went to talk to Paddy and Robbo – Ian Robertson, another Dublin star of that era, another Kickhams man through and through.

'Of course you can do it, Philly. You'd be well able for it. Let me know if you need a hand with anything.'

They had both been down this path before, and they weren't unlike me: juggling part-time jobs with club football and inter-county careers, but they still found a way to get their degrees. Paddy had gone from studying maths and physics into primary school teaching. Today he's back in Our Lady of Victories on the Ballymun Road, his old school, where he's the vice principal. Robbo studied physics as well before switching over into medicine and training up as a doctor.

After five minutes in their company, you'd have the confidence to think that you could go on to do anything. I respected and admired and trusted them, so to hear the words from their mouths, that of course I'd be able to handle a university course, it was huge for me.

As always with the two lads, they were able to help in a very practical sense as well. Turning my pretty meaningless Leaving Cert into a college place was going to be a challenge, and I didn't know where to start, but they put me in touch with Professor Niall Moyna, who was just starting out as manager of DCU's Sigerson Cup team at the time, as well as Ross Munnelly.

Ross had a great football career of his own with Laois and with the Irish international rules team and, by chance, he was working in DCU student services at the time. He was a massive help when it came to setting down the different options for me.

He sat me down in the office and talked me through it all.

'Look, Philly,' he explained, 'you've two choices here really. You can go off and wait for a couple of years, and once you turn 23, you'll be eligible to apply as a mature student and your Leaving Cert won't matter as much.

'Or,' he added, 'you can go back and repeat your Leaving Cert and if you do well enough, you'll be starting here next September.'

I didn't have any real profile as a Dublin footballer at the time, but there was a sports scholarship on the table that might make life a bit easier, Ross explained. I had my heart set on doing sports science, but when we did the sums, even when you took the scholarship into account as well, it still wouldn't give me enough points to get into that course.

That helped make my mind up. I didn't really want to go to college on the back of a sports scholarship. I wanted to do it for myself, the way most people did it. I wanted to repeat my Leaving Cert.

I sat down the following week with my parents.

'Mam, Dad ...'

I'd say they didn't know what to expect. God knows there was enough going on in our lives without me landing in with any sort of bombshell.

'I've been thinking, and I'm going to go back and repeat my Leaving Cert,' I said.

'Are you? Philip, that's great.'

That immediate reaction was the one that I was hoping for, and between the three of us, we got about 15 seconds out of it before the practicalities of what I was suggesting set in. I had a job, a job that I liked and enjoyed, a job that was paying me good money, a job that was flexible enough to support my football, and now I wanted to give it up and go back to school? Sure I never did a tap when I was in school the first time around.

My parents have always backed me 100% in everything, but Mam's tone changed to a noticeably more cautious one.

'Ah, I don't know if this is really the best idea, Philip.'

Then she said what we were both thinking, the one obstacle that I still hadn't managed to figure out for myself.

'What about your loan?'

I looked out the window to where the Audi was sitting on the side of the road, freshly polished and lit up by the last of the evening sun.

That wasn't going to stop me. We would find a way to make things work.

———

I flipped the indicator and swung off the Swords Road into the tree-lined driveway that leads you to the front door of Plunket College in Whitehall. I've been in All-Ireland finals in front of 80,000 people in Croke Park, pulled on the Irish jersey and played for my country, and sat in business meetings with hundreds of thousands, potentially millions of euros, in future revenue on the line.

But your first day in school – any school – brings a little bit of nervousness and anxiety that nothing else can match.

The first thing that hit me was how young the other students seemed. It was all in my head, of course. I was only 20, just turning 21, so I couldn't have been any more than two or three years older than those who were doing their Leaving for the first time, or those who had just tried and were back straight away to give it a second go. But I was so used to being the baby of the class for all my life, I couldn't help but notice.

As I was driving in, a couple of people walked past me in twos and threes, already friends from school probably. A few others chained their bikes to the railings and the bike racks. Some had been dropped off by their parents at the main gate.

Nobody was driving an Audi A4.

I doubt any of them even noticed that I was driving this big flashy car either, but as I looked for a parking spot, it felt like there were a thousand eyes staring at me. Every nudge and whisper took on a life of its own.

'Who's your man?'

'Dunno, a teacher maybe.'

'Bit young to be a teacher.'

'Is he loaded? Where'd he get the money for the car?'

'Dunno, probably sells drugs or something.'

In reality, these conversations were likely to have been far more mundane.

'Here, check and see if you're in my class for maths.'

'What time do we get lunch at?'

'Any idea where the jacks are in this place?'

Of course I stood out, but if there were one or two people trying to suss me out, I didn't give a shit – or at least that's what I told myself. I had paid off a good bit of the money I owed for the car, but I would have been taking a huge hit if I had tried to sell it on before going back to school. That wasn't an option, and neither was putting my life on hold for another year or two until the loan was cleared. I would have to find some way to manage.

Any hesitation that my parents felt about me going back to school stemmed from money worries. I had quit my job in DCU so that I wouldn't have any distractions. I had already done one half-assed Leaving Cert; I didn't need another one. I had become used to having money in the bank and being able to buy things when I wanted them, but once I handed in my notice I was back to being broke again, and there aren't many banks that will accept good intentions or sob stories as payments against a car loan.

The financial pressure was the biggest test of my will, tougher than any subject or exam paper. It had an impact on my parents as well, and I could see that for every sacrifice I was making, they were making double. I was sleeping under their roof and eating their food and they wouldn't take so much as a penny from me. If I pissed away this chance by not giving it everything, I wouldn't just be letting myself down; I'd be letting them down too.

I was very determined as well that they'd never think that I was taking their support for granted or abusing it. On Sunday evening, I went down to the shop and bought two things: a long pan of white bread and one of those big packets of cooked ham. I came home and made a sandwich to take with me to school the following day, and then put the rest away to do me for my sandwiches for the rest of the week. I brought €2 with me every day to buy myself a drink at lunchtime, and that was the extent of my budget. I did the same thing religiously for the entire year I was back in school. Ham sandwiches, five days a week, every week – if the nutritionist that was working with the Dublin U21s at the time had known that, I would have been in trouble. It wasn't the healthiest thing in the world, but I didn't have a choice, I was that broke.

Those struggles focused my mind as much as anything. If was putting myself through that kind of hardship, I had to make sure that it was worth it in the end. Second time around, my attitude to school had changed completely. I was still a bit of a messer – you never lose that – but I wasn't there because my parents had sent me or because it was the law. I wanted to be there and I had a goal.

Keith Cribbin, who plays football for Kildare, was repeating his Leaving Cert as well at the same time. Keith was great craic and a great footballer, and DCU were happy to help him out. The college set him up with digs on campus while he was studying for his repeats and they arranged for a grinds tutor, Sinead, to come over and give us a hand whenever we were getting stuck. She was brilliant, but old habits die hard, and I'd say the pair of us must have driven her mental with our messing.

Growing up, it had been easy for me to talk myself down and convince myself that I was academically weak and that school wasn't for me, but once I matured a bit and started to apply myself, I was as capable as anyone in the class. I never studied any science subjects the first time around, but now I signed up to take higher-level physics and chemistry, which are usually seen as two of the harder exams, and I was really good at biology because of all of the work I'd done in fitness over the years.

The biggest change of all was me realising the potential that I had. I got 420 points when I repeated my Leaving Cert a few months later, a massive improvement on my first attempt. I rang Mam and Dad. I was going to university.

———

In there with all the study notes and past exam papers, an opportunity that would ultimately change my life presented itself out of nowhere. My phone rang and on the other end was a guy looking for a coach to do a bit of strength and conditioning work with a GAA team he was training.

'We only need you for an hour,' he said. 'I'll give you 60 quid a session.'

I was drowning in ham sandwiches – surely I could manage an hour a week without letting my study go off the rails? It was too good to turn down.

Just like that I had my first clients, but I didn't have anywhere to train them. My first premises was in the attic in the Kickhams clubhouse. It wasn't a gym as such, more like a room that could be used for mobility and flexibility drills. There was a lad who used to use it to train the senior team so there were a couple of benches and weights, but that was about the sum of it. I went to the committee and explained the situation to them, and when they agreed, I went and made sure that this other fella knew who was in charge. The senior team had dropped him, but he was still using the space.

'Listen,' I said to him, 'this is my club. This is my gym now.'

The committee backed me and I'll always be grateful to them, and to men like Sean Andrews, Val's brother, who gave me the opportunity to start up my business.

For a while, that team were my only clients. Then four women got in touch to ask me if I would train them in a small semi-private session, and Philly McMahon's Bootcamp was born. The name didn't last for long, but that was the beginning of the business that has grown into three gyms across Dublin with hundreds of clients.

I could never have anticipated how quickly the business would take off. Bootcamps were still a relatively new idea in

Ireland at the time and word of mouth spread around the community. Within a year, I was looking out onto one of Ballymun Kickhams' pitches and there was a class of about 60 women all working out on a summer's evening. It was crazy, absolutely crazy.

That rate of growth would make any businessman's eyes light up – but I wasn't a businessman. I was a teenager running fitness classes out of the attic of a GAA club, and I was in way over my head. I didn't know the first thing about business, I hadn't even done business studies in school, and to make it worse, a combination of fear and thick-headedness meant that I was too afraid to ask for help. There was an incredible amount of money coming in every week and I didn't even have the sense to get an accountant. I asked my sister Kellie, who was training to be an accountant, to help me keep track of the books.

'At least you'll know which side is the money I'm making and which side is the money I'm spending,' I told her, only half-joking.

In the space of 12 months, I went from flat-out broke to making the kind of money I could only have dreamed about. I still had so much to learn though. For one thing, I knew nothing about branding and marketing. The name Philly McMahon's Bootcamp seemed quite negative to me. I didn't want people thinking that I'd be standing there and screaming my head off at them like some sort of deranged drill instructor. I save that for the football pitch. Anyway, the bootcamp concept was someone else's idea. What I was building was unique.

By this stage, I was back in DCU as a student and had started my degree in education and training. My Leaving Cert points had been good enough for a place on the sports science course, but I changed my mind at the last minute. Teaching appealed to me, but I was more interested in it from a lifestyle growth and development perspective rather than in a school. The education and training degree focused on subjects like how different people learn, how to construct courses, and how to communicate. If I was serious about turning my little start-up gym into something bigger, they were all areas that I would need to develop.

One of the modules was all about the American psychologist Howard Gardner and his theory of multiple intelligences. His idea is that there is no one ability or skillset that defines your intelligence and that there are actually eight different 'intelligences' that everybody has to a different extent. Some people are more visual, others more musical, some people are good with maths and logic while others are good with words. I was most interested in his idea of bodily-kinaesthetic intelligence, the physical control that you have over your body and the tasks that you're able to get it to perform. An elite athlete, a top inter-county GAA player, would score highly on bodily-kinaesthetic intelligence.

Out went the name Philly McMahon's Bootcamp, and in came the name BK Fitness. I intended the letters BK to stand for bodily-kinaesthetic, which I felt captured the unique approach that we were trying to take in our gym. To be fair, it probably did – but it also would have been an absolute marketing disaster. Imagine trying to explain that to a potential client or an investor in a 30-second elevator pitch.

'BK Fitness – what's that?'

'Well it stands for Bodily-Kinaesthetic Fitness. You see, there's this academic theory that there's actually no such thing as intelligence and …'

'Zzzzzzzzzz.'

I was saved from myself by pure dumb luck. Most people never even asked what the BK was, they just assumed that it stood for Ballymun Kickhams. Now that would have been good branding. I didn't bother with the real explanation.

I might not have had an accountant or a great marketing mind or any real business skills in those early days, but I knew that the only way to make the gym bigger and better was by reinvesting the money as it came in. Every time we made a few euro, I bought bits and pieces of equipment and started to kit the place out. Structurally, we started to transform the attic into a space that actually bore some resemblance to a gym. I walked in one day and one guy, an amazing man named Anto Welby, was there laying bricks.

'I'm just going to finish laying this wall first,' he told me, 'and then I'll get started on plastering that other one there after lunch.'

Anto was doing all of that work, building the walls from scratch, for free. I was overwhelmed by the support I was getting from my fellow club members in Kickhams, some really special people who were determined to help me out in whatever way they could.

Word of mouth was the most powerful advertising tool I had. The phone was ringing off the hook from different trainers within the club who were looking to book a session or two for their teams, and there were loads of outside clients coming to me directly as well. From there, the next opportunities arose. Good Counsel GAA club out in Drimnagh had a space that they wanted to offer to me. I called out to take a look. It was much smaller than the gym I had developed in Kickhams, but there was still plenty of room to make it viable. I took it, and I was still getting that one off the ground and up and running properly when Thomas Davis GAA club from Tallaght got in touch. Would I have any interest in taking over their gym?

It felt like the blink of an eye and I had gone from training four women in a nondescript attic to operating three gyms spread across the city. Whether I had planned it or not, I wasn't a fitness coach any more; I was a business owner. I couldn't be in three places at once so I had to hire staff, develop a proper budget and payroll system, and start paying wages. It wasn't as easy as stuffing rolls of twenties into my pocket and scribbling down the details in an old notebook for records any more. I had coaches running classes in my name and I had to be sure that they were doing things the right way. I needed to develop the fitness principles that I stood for and that I wanted my gyms to represent, and make sure that everyone working with me understood them and stuck to them. It was no use just having them in my head.

Again, a lot of this was trial and error. I was making plenty of mistakes, but more importantly, I was learning as I went along. While the business was exploding all around me and taking on a life of its own, I was in the middle of a three-year degree in DCU, which was challenging enough in its own right. I had managed to get past that little mental roadblock of thinking that I didn't belong in university and that I wouldn't be able to handle it academically.

I was enjoying the challenge, even thriving on it, but there came a point where I had to ask myself if it was really worth it. I had a booming gym business, which was raking in money, and I was doing really well for myself. Did I really need to finish my degree? Was I spreading myself too thin and, in the process, selling myself short? If I quit college and put all of those extra hours into developing and growing the gyms instead, how much more money could my business be making?

You could have made lots of good arguments for packing in the degree, and it certainly would have been the easy option, but nothing I had done up to that point had been the easy option. I had given up a perfectly comfortable lifestyle and career path and quit a job I liked to go back and do my Leaving

Cert. I had struggled by on little more than a tenner a week while I tried to juggle school and football. I had blocked out all of that negativity that was telling me I was crazy to even think that I could survive in a university course. If I walked away now, I could probably make more money for myself – but then all of that hardship would have been for nothing. I knew that the feeling I'd get from achieving my degree, that piece of paper that nobody can ever take away from me that says Philly McMahon is a university graduate, it would bring me much more happiness and satisfaction than any money I could make from the gym.

There's no doubt that that struggle was the deciding influence in me staying on to finish my degree. Besides, I've never really been interested in making money for money's sake anyway. My motivation has always come from the same place, whether it's in sport or education or business. I want to force myself to do the things that, at one point, I thought I could never do.

Instead of quitting, I launched myself into working on a thesis that quickly became an obsession. I was fascinated by Gardner and his intelligences theory because I could relate to it straight away. In school I was always poor at maths but good at PE, so I obviously fell into the categories of having poor logical-mathematical intelligence but good bodily-kinaesthetic intelligence. How many other kids out there were like me, or the opposite, maths geniuses but physically poor?

My thesis was all about cross-curricular development, how to teach kids maths through PE. You develop simple exercises and turn it into a game. Measuring a pitch can help with simple addition and subtraction. The shape of different pitch markings, the boxes and semi-circles, are brilliant for geometry; finally the GAA's love of the large and small parallelogram has a use. Turn a lesson about different areas and spaces into a talk about tactics and certain kids respond in a totally different way. The skill is finding a way to connect learning to enjoyment because that's what leads to engagement, and engagement is what leads to development. It was the same with me and my thesis. I was engaged with it because I enjoyed it, and so I found it easier than I ever thought I could.

I'm still a young man and I hope that I have lots more to achieve in sport and in business, and many years from now when I take stock of it all, I'll be fortunate enough to have a lot of very happy memories to reflect on.

And someday when I'm sitting there and wondering if it's all real and how it happened, I'll be able to look back on that morning in DCU.

Me and Mam and Dad standing together, where we belonged, all those moments of pressure and worry and anxiety dissolved into three proud smiles, and a university graduate in the family.

———

Football was a constant throughout those years. By the time we were playing our second year of minor in 2005, it had been 20 years since Kickhams' last county title. Whatever culture of success or winning there had once been in the club was gone.

That season Paddy arranged for us to go over to London, a team-bonding trip, and play a challenge match against a team from St Mary's University up in Strawberry Hill. It was an unbelievable trip, one of the standout memories from all of my time with Kickhams. Paddy brought four or five of the senior team with him as well, but they would have needed twice that number to keep us under control.

One of the nights after dinner, we came back to the place where we were staying and myself and a couple of the lads opened the door to our room.

'What the fuck happened here?'

Our things were all over the place, our bags emptied and stuff tossed everywhere.

While we started to put things back together again and work out what had gone missing, someone went down to get Paddy. The rest of the lads heard the racket and naturally enough stuck their heads out into the corridor to see what was going on. Anyway, Paddy was trying to work out what to do and who to call when he heard this snigger.

'Ah stop, Paddy, it's grand …'

Davey was standing outside the room next door, doubled over laughing. It turns out there was a balcony connecting the two rooms and the little bollocks had climbed out his window, in through ours, and turned the place upside down before we went out. He thought he was hilarious. We tried to do the same thing the next day and get him back, obviously, but the element of surprise was gone.

Just to make Paddy's life that little bit harder, some of the lads had already turned 18 so they were allowed to have one or two drinks while we were away, and a couple of the younger lads would have been sneaking a few as well. One of the nights, Sean Currie was feeling the effects and decided to take himself off to bed early, but when the lads got back to the room later on, he was nowhere to be seen. The manhunt got underway.

'Lads, have any of you seen Curryier? He's not here in the room.'

Eventually they gave up and decided that he must have wandered off to find more craic somewhere else. A few minutes later, they heard this purring noise that sounded like it was coming from the bathroom.

'What's that? Is there a cat after getting into the bathroom?'

When they opened the door, Curryier was sitting there in the bath, laughing his head off, delighted that his best impression of a cat had been good enough to fool the others.

We played our game against Strawberry Hill and came home, and the next week, we were out against Brigid's in the Dublin minor championship. Something clicked and we played them off the park. It wasn't just that we beat them for the first time ever, but we hammered them. Maybe the trip to London had pulled us together and made us that little bit tighter as a group. Maybe we were finally hitting the growth spurt that meant we were able to stand up to these bigger teams physically. Maybe they had taken their foot off the pedal a little bit – they certainly wouldn't have been the first team to do that at the age of 17 or 18, when drink and women and all of these other distractions start to come into play for lads. Whatever it was, we beat them out the gate and we were left looking at each other, thinking, 'Was it that easy all along?'

We didn't win the minor championship that year – Crokes beat us in the final – but there was a real sense that we had turned a corner. The only thing that could hold us back now was ourselves. It all came together two years later, in 2007.

Portmarnock. The night of the Dublin U21 championship final. Us and Na Fianna, neighbours and rivals. Eoin Dolan pulled us into the huddle for one last message before we went back out for the second half.

'We gave them enough respect out there to do for two games,' he said.

That set the standard that we all had to reach in the next few minutes. Find your man and let him know you're there. He thinks he wants to win this match, but there's no way in the world that he wants it as much as you do tonight.

They were two points up, and we were in danger of letting another county title slip through our fingers. It's easy to look back now through the old team-sheets and pick out the familiar names. Players who went on to win a Dublin championship, players who went on to play for their county, players who won All-Irelands. When Ballymun Kickhams became a force once again at senior level, these players were the backbone of the revival.

But in order for that to happen, we needed to win something. We were sick of getting back onto the bus and into the cars and talking about what we were going to do differently the next time. Every time we got close to winning a major trophy, we seemed to run into one team that was better than us.

By 2007, most of us were 19 or 20, and we were ready. We were playing with a bit of confidence, although that was nothing unusual. We had a strong core of players in the team, and good depth in the squad as well. Most importantly, we were starting to fill out. A lot of lads, myself included, had been called into Dublin development squads and been involved in minor and u21 panels at county level. When that happens, you start to want more for yourself. You start to take football a bit more seriously. You start to go to the gym. You start to eat better. Now when we came up against Crokes and Brigid's, it wasn't as easy for them to physically bully us any more.

A lot of us had a few years of senior football under our belt as well. I was only 16 when Niall O'Connell, the senior manager, brought me down for my first league game and threw me in at corner-forward against St Anne's. I don't know what people expected of me that night, but when you get that sort of responsibility at a young age, the onus is on you to step up; I kicked four points.

But the senior team weren't in a good place at all, and every year seemed to be a constant struggle just to keep our heads above water and avoid relegation. Guys like Paddy, Robbo, Stephen Condon, Darren Ducie, Dave Martin, they were still the main men, but there was a massive age gap between those older fellas and us. There were a couple of lads in between – Dec Kearns, Si Lawlor, Enda Dolan, Kev Leahy, Donie Hardiman – but other than that they were holding on for our team to come through so that we could take over. One look at the packed sidelines that night told you how much it meant for the club even to be in an U21 final.

We had plenty of great battles with that Na Fianna side over the years, but whether it was nerves or that we just weren't on our game, we didn't start well. Probably our best ever chance and we were throwing it away. There was no need for a bollocking from Paddy or Robbo or Phil O'Dea at half time. We knew that we were letting ourselves down.

With three minutes to play, we were still up against it. For a second, we switched off, and they came straight up the middle to kick a point and go one up. The heads didn't drop though. There was still time. We got an equaliser and then, in the last minute, Ted Furman was clipped as he scooped up a breaking ball. He kept his balance and the ref played advantage, and he set up Karl O'Reilly, who turned back in on his right and swung over a lovely point. We won their kickout and got another to make it safe. The party started over on the sideline, and the rest of us could finally breathe out. It had taken more than 10 years, but we'd won our county title.

It might only have been an U21 championship, but don't underestimate what it meant to that group of lads and our club. To Paddy too. Kickhams were living from season to season when he first started off with us as a bunch of eight- and nine-year-olds, and he knew that there were no quick fixes. To put the right structures in place and blood young players, it would take vision and a plan. And time. If a long game was what the club needed, he was willing to play it.

People within the club watched us coming up through the age grades and waited patiently for boys to become men. Now there was hope again. Paddy persevered and stuck with us. He could have taken the easy option and passed us on, gone back for a fresh start with another team in our place, but winning was never his priority. He wanted to develop us, to keep us playing until we eventually fed into an adult team. If that was senior, intermediate, or junior B, he didn't care.

He had a team of champions, and together we had shown the way for every youngster that was coming behind us. We went out and backed it up by winning the U21 championship again the next year, 2008. Paddy made me the captain, and I had the privilege of lifting the cup after we beat Thomas Davis in the final.

Who knows what would have happened if we had gone down fighting again in those finals? No matter how confident you are and how much belief you have in what you're doing, there will always be that tiny little doubt until you finally get over the line. It was the first serious silverware that the club had won in a long time, as long as any of us could remember anyway. It didn't dampen our appetite. If anything, it made us want even more.

———

John always made sure that I knew how proud he was of me and what I was doing, winning trophies with Kickhams and getting onto Dublin panels. He never missed an opportunity to remind me. He had his mates driven demented with the amount of stories that he wanted to tell them about me – 'My little brother Philly is doing this' or 'My little brother Philly is doing that'.

His struggles pushed me further towards football. I couldn't help him because I didn't know how, I didn't have the tools, and instead I put all of my time and energy into becoming a better player. An extra session in the gym, one last drill after training. The more I gave of myself on the pitch, the less time I had to worry about everything else that was going on at home.

But football was more than just a distraction. It became the most important part of who I was. While people I knew were going to jail or getting caught up in drugs, it was football and my ability that saved me from that. When you're competing for a place on a county panel, at any age, the stakes are high and the margins are fine, but if I didn't have football, I had nothing. It was the key that opened doors that would have been bolted shut otherwise. Realistically, without football, there was no gym, there was no business. Nobody cared about Philly McMahon from Ballymun, but Philly McMahon the Dublin footballer? That was different.

When I was dropped by Pat Gilroy in 2009, it was not only the biggest setback of my sporting career, it was one of the toughest challenges of my life.

Did you ever get that feeling when your heart goes 100 miles an hour and your stomach just sinks? That's the only way I can describe it. I put down the phone and stared at the wall, as if that was where I would find an explanation that made sense. Because at that moment, nothing made sense to me.

I made my senior Dublin debut under Pillar Caffrey in 2008, but when Pat took over at the end of that year and started to put his panel together for the new season, I found out that I wasn't part of his plans. Devastating doesn't even begin to sum it up.

I rang him to get an explanation.

From the moment he picks up the phone, you're battling to keep your emotions in check. It's nearly impossible to do that, but they're about the only thing that you can control in this situation. Apart from that, you're powerless. You get angry, even though you know the anger won't change his mind. You argue your case as though there's actually something to be talked through and discussed, when really the decision has been made and nothing that you say is going to change that.

Pat's a businessman. He's had hundreds of conversations like this and he knows how to handle them. He says all the things that you'd expect him to say.

'Go back to your club and we'll keep an eye on you.'

That's no consolation when you have to hang up the phone, walk into the next room, and tell your family that you're no longer a Dublin player. That part of your life that has made everybody so proud and so happy is gone. It was the exact same feeling that I felt when lads were sneering in my face, telling me that my brother was a junkie. You can't begin to imagine what that embarrassment is like. You do not want to talk to anybody about anything. It is hell, pure depression.

Dropped.

It's more than just a word; it's what it represents – a failure in your sporting career, which, at that time, was the foundation for my entire world. If you are privileged enough to play for your county, that is how people see you and relate to you. Once you're on that panel, you're a Dublin footballer first and foremost, and everything else is secondary after that. When you meet your friends, or you're out at a family gathering, or when someone stops you on the street, football is usually the first place they go to – how are you set for Sunday, or how's training going, or how's so and so getting on with the injury?

Once you've been cut loose from the squad like that, it feels like there's only one conversation in your life, and it's playing over and over again on a loop. It clings to you, and if you're not careful, it becomes part of how you think about yourself.

'Are you playing at the weekend?'

'No, I'm not on the team any more.'

'What happened?'

'I got dropped.'

'Why did you get dropped?'

'I don't actually know. I was told to go back to the club.'

It had happened to me once before, in 2007, two nights before making my championship debut for the Dublin U21s.

We're up in the Trinity grounds in Santry for our final training session before we play Meath, and Paddy Canning, the manager, pulls me aside. In my mind, I'm thinking that he's coming over with a little bit of advice, maybe something he knows about the lad that I'm marking on Saturday afternoon. What he's actually about to say to me isn't even on my radar.

'Listen, Philly, you're not part of the panel for the day and …'

I'm stunned. I think it takes a few minutes for me to actually realise that he's said 'not part of the panel'. It's not complacency. I've been in the half-forward line for every one of our challenge games, and now this? I've gone from sure-fire starter in my head to not even being on the bench. Not only am I not one of the top 15 players here – are you telling me that I'm not even in the top 26?

I hadn't the first clue about how I should be dealing with it. I did all the wrong things. I went back out into the next drill and my head was still spinning. I was looking at all of the other lads – my teammates – and picking holes in their games and finding fault. Who is he going to start ahead of me? I couldn't see a single person who was good enough to take my place.

Then I went and doubled down on that negativity. When Paddy named the team, I went straight to the lads who were due to be on the bench. It was totally subconscious but my confidence had taken such a massive hit, my instinct was to connect with people who would reassure me that Paddy had got it wrong. All I wanted was for them to massage my ego and tell me that I should have been playing. I wasn't mature enough to take a step back and try to see things from Paddy's perspective, to ask if it had been a tactical decision, or to look at how I'd been playing myself in training and in challenge matches, to see if I could have done more. Anger and frustration clouded everything, and it only made matters worse.

We lost by four points. My first U21 championship was over before I even got a chance to kick a ball.

That night, we went to a place called Barcode. It doesn't exist any more, but it was one of those nightclubs that everybody of a certain age from the northside of Dublin would know. Bizarrely enough, it was actually part of a big gym in Fairview. After you'd got your ID checked by the security, you'd walk in past the swimming pool to get into the club, and it'd be hard to say what was more overpowering – the bang of Brylcreem and dodgy teenage aftershave or the chlorine. So weird really, but we thought it was amazing when we were younger. It was the place to be if you weren't going into town.

We were all in brutal form after losing, but I was worse than anybody, sulking with a big thick head on me. Every conversation I had was the same. The lads who didn't start were asking questions. The lads who started were asking questions. Everyone was asking questions, and I was getting more and more angry that I didn't have any answers for them. I already felt hard done by, but this was only winding me up even more. I was so frustrated, I just walked out. Left the lads there to play their few games of pool and have a drink and a dance and forget about it. I couldn't forget about it.

For 10 years, people had been telling me that I had talent, that I had ability, that I was as good as anyone else out there and, let's be honest, better than most of them. I just had to keep my head down, stay out of trouble, and work at being the best I could be. The rest would fall into place.

Well, it wasn't fucking falling into place, was it? Once you stop feeling sorry for yourself, that's when you start to ask questions. The little doubts start nipping away at your confidence. Am I really good enough to play for Dublin? Because the man who makes that decision, the man whose job it is to decide who is good enough and who is not, he doesn't think I am. Not even good enough that he might want to use me as Plan B or C or D, a last roll of the dice when there's nothing left to lose.

But all of my life, I've had people telling me what I can and can't do, and I've never listened to any of them. I wasn't backing down from a fight. When the team was picked for the first round of the u21 championship in 2008, my name was in the starting xv – but it wasn't Paddy Canning reading it out. He had stepped down at the end of his three-year term and the county board had brought in a new face to replace him.

Jim Gavin needed no introduction: one of the stars of that famous All-Ireland winning team in 1995 and a man who had already tasted success at this level. He had been one of the coaches when Dublin won the u21 All-Ireland under Tommy Lyons in 2003, and now he was back to do it again. Jim must have seen some leadership potential in me because he made me captain. It was an incredibly proud moment for me, and a little bit of vindication, but our championship campaign was over just as quickly again. We lost to Kildare by a point.

Those major examples of adversity in my life – being dropped by Paddy Canning at u21s, coming to terms with John's addiction, and then being dropped by Pat Gilroy – the process for dealing with them was very similar. Some of them were bigger obstacles than others, of course, but the feelings were the same, and if I hadn't experienced them, I wouldn't have developed that strength of character that allowed me to move on from the next one and the next one.

Pat was well within his rights to drop me if he felt that was what was best for the team, but there was no point in looking for someone to blame. When I thought about it, I knew that there was only one person who could change his mind: me. If I wasn't getting picked, that was my own fault. If I didn't play, I must have been doing something wrong or there must have been more I could have done. That became my goal in sport: to get the jersey and keep the jersey. If that was the focus in my training and in my performance, I'd be giving my all for the team as well. Everything else would flow from that.

It's no coincidence that my best ever season with Ballymun was in 2009, the year that I was dropped. I went back with a vengeance, determined not to be forgotten. Declan Sheehan was the manager at that stage, and he had me in at full-back where I was playing some of the best football of my career. We won the league, our first Division 1 title since the 1980s, which was huge for us. After the back-to-back u21 successes, winning was starting to become a habit.

It was only much later that I found out that I had an offer to go to America that summer. One of the teams in Boston had heard that I was dropped by Dublin and they were scouting around for players to go and play in their championship. The usual offer was on the table. They'd look after the flights and the accommodation for as long as you were over there playing, and there'd be a good job in it for you as well with a decent chunk of money.

Not going to America probably turned out to be one of the key decisions in my football career – except it wasn't my decision. When the Boston club rang Ballymun so that they could chat to me about it, the lad who took the call conveniently forgot to pass on the message. They didn't want to lose me for the rest of the Dublin championship so he just said nothing. It was only months later, after we'd been knocked out, that it was ever mentioned.

That autumn, Pillar phoned.

'They've asked me to take the Leinster team for the Railway Cup this year. Would you be up for coming down?'

We were already out of the club championship, beaten by Crokes in the quarter-finals. I said yes.

It was a huge confidence boost for me. When a new manager comes in at county level, it should be a fresh start for everyone, except I never got a fresh start when Pat took the Dublin job. But there are very few players out there who are playing for their province and not for their county, so I seized on that. The issue with Dublin obviously wasn't about my ability.

Our game was against Ulster, in Crossmaglen's place up in Armagh. You couldn't play football in the wind. Gary Connaughton from Westmeath was playing in goal for us, and every time he tried to kick the ball out in the second half, it was getting caught and nearly landing back in his hands. That day I marked Stephen O'Neill, Benny Coulter, and Michael Murphy, three of the best players on the pitch and three of the most talented footballers to come out of Ulster in the last 20 years. Between them, they managed one point from play.

We still lost though. Ulster got a huge run on us in the second half when they had the wind at their backs and there was

The siblings: June, me, Lindy, Kellie and John. Judging by the egg in John's hands, this was probably taken around Easter 1989. I was, and still am, the baby of the family.

It feels like I spent most of my childhood outside, thumping footballs off the walls and kerbs of our neighbourhood. Later on it would become a way to sneak closer to John, but here I'm just getting started.

This is the Ballymun I remember. John (L) is wearing his Everton kit, his friend Derek has his Liverpool tracksuit on, while Dad and I sit between them. This was taken on the hill outside the flats. When we got older, we'd use it as a tee box and launch golf balls into Glasnevin. We had a flat just like the one behind us. To get home, we'd climb through the windows rather than walk around the block.

John and I were really close from the beginning. The years that followed weren't always easy, but we never lost that connection.

Caffo and Young Caffo, aka John (R) and me.

I never knew John played football in school – he wasn't big into sport – until I spotted a familiar face in this photo on a wall in our old primary school, Holy Spirit in Ballymun. There he is in the back row, second from the right, looking like he's up to mischief.

Ballymun always felt more like a family than a town or part of a big city. Here, John (L) and Mossy's ma Sandra – who always let me stay for dinner! – help my sister Kellie, in purple, off to her debs.

John and Val on the day of his confirmation. Mam and Dad never lost sight of the real John, even when things got really difficult.

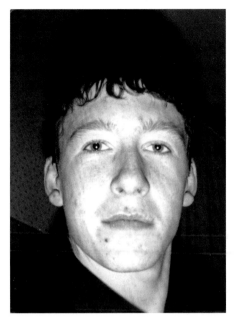

For a time, John managed to hide his problems from the rest of the family. He can't have been more than 14 or 15 when this photo was taken, but he'd already tried hard drugs. The cycle of addiction that would define the rest of his life had already begun.

Growing up, Carl Corcoran (L) was one of John's closest friends. We all loved him. Like others in John's circle, he started dabbling in drugs at a young age. He got clean for a time and moved away from Ballymun, tried to move on with his life, but one slip killed him. It felt like a final warning.

Me, Lindy and John on his last Christmas with the family in 2011. We knew John was struggling, but we didn't know how badly. As ever, he tried his best to put us at ease and keep us laughing.

Davey, me and Dad at the Kickhams awards night. Kickhams has always been about more than football: it's a family, a support system, a sense of purpose. It gave us somewhere to go and something to focus on other than the streets. We may have changed but the club never did.

Dad with some of Paddy Christie's Dublin gear. Paddy's giveaways and coaching kept us focused on what could be achieved if we kept working hard. Croke Park was a long way off, but it wasn't impossible.

I've always been incredibly proud to wear the red and green. The club has given me so much: friends and advice, the Dubs, my start in business. (© INPHO/James Crombie)

Winning the Leinster Senior Club Championship with Kickhams so soon after John's death was one of the proudest moments of my life. It inspired me to look at life differently. Here I am after the match with our manager Paul Curran (C), Derek Byrne, Elliott Reilly and Tommy Hennessy. (© David Maher/SPORTSFILE)

My last visit to the towers was in 2015, a few days after the All-Ireland final. It felt like I'd come full circle. After it came down, all we were left with was memories. (© Brenda Fitzsimons/Irish Times)

I'm often told there are two Phillys: the guy on the pitch – physical, aggressive – and everyday Philly, who's pretty much the opposite. It's tough to explain why this is, but I know playing for Dublin gives me the platform to do everything I want in life, from growing my businesses to starting my own charity. It's the key to everything, so I can't afford not to push myself to the limit. There have been times when I've gone too far and done things I've regretted, but I'll never apologise for trying. (Above: © INPHO/Donall Farmer; below: © Piaras Ó Mídheach/ SPORTSFILE)

I've changed a lot about the way I think and play these last few years, but my celebrations haven't changed much. I might need to work on that.

(© INPHO/Ryan Byrne)

(© INPHO/Ryan Byrne)

(© David Maher/SPORTSFILE)

(© INPHO/Cathal Noonan)

In the four years since we started going out, Sarah has been one of the most positive forces of change in my life. She's an incredible person. This was taken at the 2016 All-Star Ceremony. (© Ramsey Cardy/SPORTSFILE)

I know it doesn't exactly fit with my reputation, but I thought long and hard about going to art school.

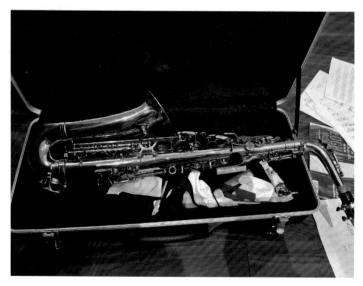

My saxophone, awaiting the All-Ireland jam session with Kev McManamon.

nothing we could do. You might think it's only the Railway Cup, it doesn't matter, but apart from the club All-Ireland, it's the only medal I don't have.

———

Every Dublin fan knows where they were for that Kerry game in 2009. There's no escaping it.

I was in the Hogan Stand – for most of the game anyway. A couple of days later, somebody showed me a photograph, a line of fans walking up the steps, the smart comments from the Kerry fans ringing in their ears.

'Cheerio, cheerio.'

'Make sure ye beat the traffic home, lads.'

And there I am, at the top of the steps, looking back over my shoulder one last time as if to confirm that this was actually happening. Snap. Sneaking out early, caught on camera by one of the photographers.

I had seen enough.

Dublin hadn't beaten Kerry in the All-Ireland in 30-something years, since the Heffo days, but this felt like the worst one of them all. A sold-out Croke Park on the August bank holiday Monday. No need for a double-header, we'd fill the place ourselves. A quarter-final but a ticket scramble as if it was the All-Ireland final itself. Listening to the way some people were talking that week, you'd think Kerry were in crisis. They'd lost to Cork, and they hadn't really set the world on fire in the qualifiers, but it wasn't like they'd forgotten how to kick a ball. Dublin had won another Leinster, the five-in-a-row, in Pat's first season. People looked at the form and saw what they wanted to see.

Kerry got a goal with their very first attack. It took less than 40 seconds, and very quickly, it was clear that all the pre-match talk had been complete hype and nonsense. Pat tried to make changes to stop the bleeding but nothing worked. He famously said afterwards that the players were like startled earwigs. It was the only way he could make sense of it.

I couldn't watch any more. I was too angry, halfway home by the time it finished Kerry 1–24 Dublin 1–7. A 17-point defeat.

Where do we go from here?

# HALF
# TIME

## My addiction

*My addiction feels like a big fat lie.*
*Sometimes I just want to lay down and die.*
*Then some days alls I do is cry, cry, cry.*
*My mother keeps on asking why, why, why.*

*I always thought I was in control*
*But I never knew I was falling into the big black hole.*
*I could feel it getting very cold.*
*Now I know the devil has my soul.*

*That's what I get for being clever.*
*Now I know I will be here forever.*
*If I ever get a second chance,*
*I will never give drugs another glance.*

*Now I know I can walk around,*
*I will never have to keep my head down.*
*Now I know I can stop the old insanity,*
*And restart my life with a new reality.*

John Caffrey

———

Carl's death felt like a final warning. If we didn't do something drastic to get John clean, we were going to be the ones standing at a graveside before too long.

Carl was a very good friend of John's growing up, one of those lads who was a little bit older than him, but someone who he always hung around with. I loved Carl too. Like the rest of us, he was crazy and a bit of a messer, but he was a good lad. The days that John brought me into town to go shopping, Carl would be there, and if there was a row between me and John, he'd step in as the mediator and get us to kiss and make up, or at least to stop bashing each other in the middle of Henry Street.

Carl was no different to John and the rest of that group, and from a young age, he started to dabble in drugs too. He was able to get himself clean, and for a long time, he did quite well. He moved away from Ballymun and moved on with his life. One slip killed him. His dad walked into the sitting room the next day and found Carl dead from an overdose.

I stood in the church that day, like I have so many times over the years, and I was terrified. Was this how it was all going to end?

At that stage a lot of my friends were starting to get mixed up in drugs as well, and Ballymun felt dangerous. All of these young lads my age grew up looking at John and the lads that he hung around with and saw them all strung out on heroin, and they laughed it off. Junkies. We'll never end up like that. And they didn't realise that they were on the same pathway in life, doing the exact same thing.

They didn't want to be in school and dropped out early. They couldn't find jobs or, if they did, they couldn't hang on to them. Instead, every new day started and ended on the blocks.

Whatever dreams they once had were pried from their fingers. Drugs became the escape, the answer to their problems, the only thing that bound them together and made them feel like they belonged. When I was with Kickhams or with Dublin, I found friends who supported each other, drove each other on, pushed each other higher and higher. A lot of young people in Ballymun had nothing like that. Nobody was looking out for them.

I couldn't understand the cycle, couldn't wrap my head around how the same thing was happening over and over again, these people that I knew, dying in their bedrooms, on their couches, on their doorsteps. Every day was a wake-up call, except nobody was fucking waking up. They were still taking drugs. They were still killing themselves. Within a couple of years, two of my friends had overdosed and died.

There was no point in us pretending that John was somehow different. He wasn't. We had tried everything and nothing was working. If it wasn't heroin, it was methadone, and then inevitably back to heroin again. It felt like he was slowly walking himself into his own grave.

Mam got a huge fright when Carl died. She didn't want to send John to England, and she wouldn't have done it if she felt that there was any other way, but we were running out of ideas and, we worried, running out of time. The only move we had left was to get him out of the country, to disconnect him completely from that part of his life and allow him to get clean and start over away from all of the temptations and 'just one' hits.

The place that he moved into over there was lovely, a beautiful apartment in this really nice estate in London. It was my cousin Derek's, and it was kitted out with everything that he could have wanted and more, TVs in every room, that kind of place, a million miles from the halfway houses and hostels that he'd been bouncing between at home.

Derek had moved back to Ireland with work at the time and so John had the run of the whole apartment to himself. All Derek asked him to do was not to wreck the place while he was gone.

'Nobody even knows I live here,' Derek said to John. 'I come and go and do my own thing, which is the way I want to keep it.' That was it.

We thought it was our breakthrough. Mam did everything she could to help John get settled in and set up. She sent him over money every week so that he could pay for food and pay his bills and he wouldn't be under pressure to find work. She didn't want him to have to go anywhere or do anything, just put all of his energy into getting himself right again.

She spent countless hours, days, maybe even months of her life in airports going over and back to visit John, checking up on him to make sure he was alright, and just to be with him and spend time with him. There were mornings when you'd hear the front door closing behind her, four o'clock, and she would be gone on her way to catch the first flight.

When John went to London initially, it was a bit of a relief. I didn't have to worry that I might run into him on the streets, or that he might show up somewhere unexpectedly and embarrass me. He only came home once a year, for a couple of days around Christmas, so we all tried to go over to visit him at different stages. Every time Mam went to see him, he was plaguing her with questions about when we would be over.

I only ever managed to get to London once. He had been living there for about a year, maybe a year and a half, at that stage, and although he wasn't working and still hadn't managed to get clean, he was doing OK for himself. We had a great few days, just doing all the things you do when life is normal – wandering around the city, doing a bit of shopping, going out for a nice meal.

Sitting in the airport waiting for my flight home, all I could think about was how lonely he seemed and how much he must have been struggling over there by himself, fighting his battle, while life went on for the rest of us back home in Dublin. He never really came to terms with that. He was too disconnected. London wasn't Dublin, and it certainly wasn't Ballymun. It was a big impersonal city of millions, and no matter how often we visited or how many hours Mam spent on the phone to him, he had nobody to lean on. No friends, no family, just long and lonely days and very little he could do to fill the time. He needed to be around people.

He was still caught in that same trap. When he moved over to London, he was on methadone treatment, and the first challenge he faced was to get connected to the right type of services over there, which wasn't always the easiest thing. Before long, the same situations started to unfold again, because as powerful as they are, it's not just the chemical hooks of the drug that keeps a person addicted, it's the societal hooks as well. If you're using methadone, nobody is going to rent you a flat or give you a job. It's the same in London as it is in Dublin – the only people who won't brush you to one side or treat you like shit are other addicts. You're in it together. It wasn't hard for John to find out who these people were or where they hung out, even in a brand new city. Before long, he was back in the thick of the exact same problems we'd tried so hard to get him away from.

Over the years, John had started to drift away from his original group of friends back home and started to hang around with more of the lads who were my age. He had become so used to being the big fish in the small pond, and he tried to create that for himself in London. He thought he could be the big man in the estate, the Irish guy that everyone was mates with and loved, and he started to gather this group of friends around him.

Derek's apartment became a place for them to hang out, and hanging out meant drink and drugs. Of course John never said a word, and let on that he was keeping up his end of the bargain with Derek, but every time Mam went over to visit, the apartment was getting that bit grubbier and something else would have broken or have gone missing. If she asked John, he always had an explanation – he had dropped the lamp when he was moving it, or that TV had never worked since he got there. At first, you would have barely noticed the damage but it quickly began to accumulate. They were wrecking the place.

Once he fell in with that group, trouble was never far away. When John rang home, he'd always have a story or two about the latest row. You started to recognise the same names over and over again, and it was rarely in a good way. The problem with John was you'd never know what to believe. Mam used to always say that half of it was true and not to mind the other half, but it was trying to work out which half was which. He was a natural-born storyteller, and a lot of the time, the truth crossed the line into fiction. Such and such had got nicked for this, or so and so had been involved in a fight. It seemed that they were always getting into fights. Day after day of binges on drink and whatever else certainly didn't help.

John got caught up in a row one night. They went back to one of these parties and a lad, a British soldier, a paratrooper, was there. Whatever was said or however it kicked off, this guy was badly hurt. A weapon was used. When the police started asking questions and taking statements, anybody they spoke to as a witness remembered the 6'4" lad in the room who stuck out like a sore thumb. Three of them were convicted, including John. He spent the next five years in jail.

———

*Alright Ma,*

*Well, back in Pentonville. The wing I'm on is a crap wing. There's too many on it, about 300–400 blokes on it. The only good thing about it, I know a few from Enfield and Tottenham so I'm alright, and my cell mate Power is OK. He's fuckin huge. How do ye think he got name Power? From power-lifting weights, and he's well known in here so that's a good thing.*

*So my number's on the top of this. Make sure ye write to me. I wanna say thanks for the Christmas we had. I had a good time. I'm sorry for acting like a prick some of the time. But we had a good laugh, I think. Tell them all I'm doing alright. I was going mad I didn't get to talk to them all the day after my birthday but at least I got to talk to Phil on Sunday. I don't know why it cut off 'cause I still had a bit of credit on it.*

*So I got that £10 off the Irish commission but they said they couldn't send me in the clothes I wanted 'cause I'm a convicted prisoner. They were going to send in a tracksuit, socks and boxers. It's a load of bollocks the way they run this place. I tell ye, if they said I could go back to Belmarsh, I'd be gone in a second. I'd love to be back there, I never thought I'd say that about a prison.*

*[...]*

*I'll write the address on the back of the envelope. Make sure ye get them all to write to me. I don't know when or how long of this sentence I'm going to do. Some are saying you get a review after 28 days. I know ye get one for definite after six months. As long as I don't get any charges, I could get out. We'll see what happens.*

*So Ma, I'll leave it there for now. I'll write every week and, again, thanks for letting me have a great Xmas. I won't*

*forget it. I just hope I get out for Philly's 21st and tell him
well done on the Dublin game, won't be long till he's on the
big stage.*

*So Ma, can't wait to hear from ye. I won't start telling ye
I'm going to do it all great and go straight 'cause ye'll say
yeah I've heard that before. So I won't say it, not yet. Anyway
Ma, ye know I love ye, Ma. Talk to you soon.*
*All my love,*
*John*

———

Belmarsh is no joke. It is one of the toughest prisons in
England, Category A, maximum security, and you're
mixing with some of the most hardened criminals in the
country. John spent most of his sentence there, although he did
have a stretch in Pentonville, another one of the London jails,
for a while as well.

It's hard to know how he coped in prison. Mam went over to
visit him every time she could and when he called home or
wrote letters to us, which was all the time, they were always
very positive, although even if he was struggling, he would
never let us see that. His letters were full of love and compassion
and, most of all, regret. He learned from his mistake, and while
he still struggled with drugs after his release, he never went
back to prison.

When he first went in, I don't think he imagined that he
would be locked up for as long as he was. He clung on to the
news of every hearing, every possible review of his case, with
the optimism of a man who thought he would be free again
sooner rather than later. Maybe that was his way of getting

through it. John was the type of person who would make a mistake, and it was only afterwards that he would think, 'What did I do that for?'

He was very political and that came out even more when he was living in England, and especially during the years when he was in prison. We'd get these letters in the post from him, decorated all around the edges with tricolours and Republican slogans.

I remember the day when Dad discovered his tattoo. He grabbed a hold of him.

'What the fuck is that on your arm?'

Dad had warned all of us never to get them and John had managed to keep this one hidden for long enough. He took one look at it.

'Oh Jesus Christ.'

An AK47 and a tricolour.

Before John left to go to London, Dad told him to keep it covered up.

'You see that there, they'll take heed of that and do something on you,' he said.

The tattoo turned out to be a bit of a blessing in disguise when he was in prison. Being Irish in the British system was a double-edged sword. John stood out because of where he was from, and got a rough time over it, but there were a lot of inmates who took one look at his arm and decided that it would be safer not to mess with him. Just in case.

When he wasn't writing letters, he was writing poetry. He wrote about what he knew – proper working-class stuff, people and their problems, his life, his addiction. It wasn't polished, it had that gritty edge to it – written in the same way as he talked, full of curse words and slang. It became his calling card in prison. The other inmates would see him writing and they'd get him to write poems about them and their stories; they would swap him a couple of cigarettes in return and take John's poem, neatly folded, back to their cell.

Sometimes he'd tuck a poem or two in with his letters to us. I was never great for writing back to him. I always preferred talking to him on the phone if I could, although I wasn't great at that either. Mam still has most of those letters and poems stored away in a box at home. I have one too. It's in a frame on my mantelpiece, hidden behind a photo of me and him and Dad in happier times.

———

*Alright Ma,*

*Well as you know, I was up in court on Tuesday and got bail.*
*[…]*
*Ma, I know you'll try your best as you said on the phone, and if you get it, running is the last thing on my mind so don't worry about that. It's just sitting down here in this block knowing I could be out on the road, it does fuck your head a bit, and I know it's my fault for being down here in the block in the first place, but you know it's for that piss test back in January so it's not like I've done anything new wrong.*

*So I've been down here 10 days. It's hard having no tobacco, no TV, no kettle, and no canteen. Alls I get is prison food. That's it. More weight I'm losing I don't need. So I'm only smoking probably three roll ups a day, some days none, and if someone gets sent down the block and has some burn. I ain't going to lie but my head is wrecked now that I've got bail. I'm just thinking what could be.*
*[…]*

*Anyway, enough of that. How are you? Hope you're alright. I'm going to ring you tomorrow and see what's up. Other than all that bail shit, I'm grand. Even though I'm down the block, I have a few mates. You don't get to see them but we all talk out the windows.*

*So your birthday's coming up. I have stuck a card in with this. Tell Kellie I couldn't get hers 'cause they have none but I'll see next week. So I hope you enjoy the day even under the circumstances. Have a great day and I'll be thinking of you.*

*So I have a few days left down here, done it like a soldier. So Ma, hope to see you soon, love you as always and never forget, Ma, whatever happens, I'll always have you close to me. Why is it that when I fuck up, you're always there for me? Whatever happens, Ma, I'll repay you for everything you've done for me.*

*So this is where I sign off for now. Hope to see you soon and, as always, I love you to bits. Stay safe and hang in there. Love,*
*Jonny Boy*

———

Even in those years when he was in prison, John never lost touch with my football career and how I was getting on. He told me stories about the rows he had with the prison guards, trying to get them to find matches on the TV or the radio in the common room on a Sunday afternoon. When I was brought back in to the Dublin squad ahead of the 2010 season, he was nearly happier than I was.

After that Kerry defeat in 2009, Dublin football had nowhere to hide; big changes needed to be made. Some of the older lads moved on, Ciarán Whelan retired, and Pat Gilroy brought in a lot of new faces. I was one of them.

Pat was very clear about what he wanted from me. He knew that it was too easy to get at Dublin, that we were too open and giving teams too much freedom. If we were going to be contenders, we needed to start by building a solid defence – but not just defence at the back. Pat wanted us to defend from the front, with the full-forward line working as hard as anyone else on the pitch when we didn't have the ball. If we got that right, it would funnel back through the rest of the team.

I was brought back in because I was tough. True to his word, he had kept an eye on me when I went back to the club, and he saw what I could bring to a Dublin full-back line. Pure determination and fight. Get your man, stick to him, and don't give him a sniff. Relentless for 70 minutes.

When I joined the squad, I could see that Pat had taken the tactical side of the game to a whole new level compared to what Pillar had been doing in 2008. The entire dynamic of the team had changed. Pat took all of his business experience and applied it. He had built and managed successful teams in the past in a different environment, and he could use all of those strategies to get more out of us. The culture changed, and not in some abstract way. He brought in structures to define who we were and how we behaved, both on and off the pitch. Nobody would be able to look at this group any more and say, as they had in the past, that we were a team of individuals.

There was a new intensity to everything we did. People looking in from the outside were obsessed with the things Pat had us doing, the 6am training sessions, Dollymount Strand in the hail, rain, or snow, pushing ourselves on pitches that were rock solid. He had his reasons, but I saw it as a test. How would lads react? Would they buy into it? Were they ready to go that extra mile in their commitment?

It wasn't just for show. We got so much out of all of those extra sessions and the hours in the gym, knowing that while other teams were still tucked up in bed, we were out in the freezing cold, trying to push our bodies and our minds to places that we weren't even sure existed.

———

Sometimes you think you're on the right track, and then something happens that forces you to take a step back and reassess. The day that we lost to Meath in 2010, the Leinster semi-final, was a weird day. A weird, weird day. It's hard to say that a result isn't a fair reflection on any match because, at the end of it all, the final score is the final score, and if you're on the wrong end of it, it's because the other team did something that you didn't. When the scoreboard says 5–9 to 0–13, there's no hiding from it.

That game was a reality check, absolutely. How could it not be? But there was never any talk of us going back to the drawing board or ripping up the plan and starting again. There was no crisis of confidence. When we broke it all down and analysed it, obviously something had gone wrong, but it wasn't a systems failure. We had changed something that day, and we certainly weren't playing with the same structure that we had before.

It was only my second championship start for Dublin. The first had come a fortnight earlier against Wexford when Pat had put me in at corner-back, part of a new-look defence along with Mick Fitzsimons and Rory O'Carroll. It's funny the things that stick in your memory. I couldn't tell you who scored the goals or kicked the points against Meath, but I remember that we got changed in the Cusack Stand dressing room for some reason, which was unusual, and I remember the heat. Ireland was in the middle of the two-day heatwave that we get every year and call a summer, and it felt like the sun was coming into Croke Park through a magnifying glass. I was that hot on the pitch that I literally started to shake, mini little convulsions. I think that was my body's way of trying to create sweat and cool itself down.

When you concede five goals in a game, the review session is always going to be a difficult place. We were beaten by 11 points in the end, but it wasn't one-way traffic from the first minute to last. Far from it. It was still level up until about the 40th minute, and we were on top in midfield for most of the game. Meath didn't even do anything particularly inventive to cut us open. We made silly individual mistakes that gave them chances and they took all of them.

Being a defender on a day like that is a nightmare, and twice as painful when you're only new to the squad and trying to nail down the jersey for yourself. I didn't need anybody to tell me I'd had a bad day. I'm my own toughest critic, and what I see and analyse in my own game is different to how others see it. I wasn't happy.

The knee-jerk reaction would have been to look at the defence and try to find the root of the trouble there, but when we looked deeper and saw where the goals had come from, we got a much clearer understanding of the mistakes that we'd made. Poor communication, people not chasing back or putting their deliveries under pressure, shots that they should never have been able to get off. It was massive shock, and a really tough result to take, but we didn't need to start from scratch. We just needed to go back to what we had been working on.

That's the good thing about the structure of the All-Ireland championship and the qualifiers. If you're beaten at that stage, you have a chance to respond immediately and rectify it. We lost to Meath on the last Sunday of June, and we were back out again a fortnight later against Tipperary in the second round of the qualifiers.

Even in the bad years, there's always a sense of expectation from Dublin fans. It's just in their nature. But that was completely wiped away after the Meath game. Dublin teams are used to running out into a wall of noise for a championship game, 50,000 or 60,000 in Croke Park even on the quiet days. When we came out of the tunnel against Tipp, you could nearly hear the sound of people zipping up their jackets in the stand. It was a Saturday night and the rain was whipping in on top of them, which didn't help, but there were only 22,000 there. We were used to seeing a sea of blue jerseys; now all we had was a sea of blue seats. It wasn't much better when we played Armagh a week later, maybe a couple of thousand more, but it's safe to say that a fairly routine win against a Tipp side we were always expected to beat hadn't exactly done much to restore confidence.

Whenever I get asked to pick a standout moment or two from my career, that Armagh game is one that my mind is always drawn to. Anyone who was there that day has probably buried the memory, which shouldn't have been hard to do. It wasn't a great game by any standards, but it was a big win for us in terms of character and confidence.

It was scrappy, a real back-and-forth but with no real excitement. They played well for a spell and went a few points up before letting us back into it; then we did the same thing. We were only a point up inside the last 10 minutes and Armagh started to come at us. I was on the edge of the square, last man back except for Clucko, and I could see the danger unfold. We had been dragged out of position and lost our shape, and there was nobody to pick up Brian Mallon. Jamie Clarke floated a ball inside that cut us open, and I wasn't close enough to get across and close down the shot. Clucko knew it instinctively and went out to narrow the angle. I dropped onto the line to cover him and thankfully, when Mallon hit his shot, it was within reach. I threw a leg in its general direction and got my toe on the end of it. I never should have got it near it – nine times out of 10, you'd miss it and it would go in – so it was a massive confidence boost for me, even more so because we only won the game by three points in the end.

Beating Armagh was a turning point in that season, and maybe in the context of what came afterwards as well. If Mallon had scored that goal, Armagh would have gone two points up and could well have kicked on and beaten us. On the back of the Kerry defeat in 2009, we then would have been hammered by Meath in a Leinster semi and lost in the third round of the qualifiers the following season. That would have been seriously tough to take, and it's very hard to know how we would have reacted as a team. Thankfully we never had to find out.

———

I had pegged Cork as All-Ireland contenders since the start of the season in 2010. They beat us comfortably enough in the league, and all the way through, they had the look of a team that was going well. If you look at the players they had, there was a really good mix of big powerful men who wanted to run the ball a lot, fast players like Paul Kerrigan and Daniel Goulding, skilful players like Paddy Kelly.

There was a break in play and I looked up at the screen. Four minutes left in an All-Ireland semi-final and we were two points up. We could be in the final in a few minutes, I thought to myself. That was my biggest mistake. I had switched my focus from the process to the outcome. From that day on, I swore I'd never think about how long was left in a game again.

Part of that comes with maturity as a footballer. Now, I have a thing in my head where I want the referee to play an extra 10 minutes all the time. I don't want the game to end. But when you're young or in the early part of your career, it's easy to think: I've done well here, I've marked my man, he hasn't done much, let the game be over before that changes.

I remember playing a challenge match when I was younger, also against Cork by coincidence. The lad who was playing corner-back alongside me started to freak me out. Every time the ball went out of play or down the other end, he'd start to drift over closer to me.

'Philly, what's left?'

He was so nervous, he kept saying it to me. 'What's left? What's left?'

He'd said it so many times, I had to ask him if he was alright. Of course he wasn't alright, he was all over the shop.

I don't want games to end. I want them to last. I want to enjoy them. I want to embrace them. But the stakes were different that day against Cork, and it was the first time I'd ever been in a position like it.

Before I knew it, the game had slipped away from us. These big monsters started running directly at us and we panicked. I know I panicked a bit. Going for a ball, Colm O'Neill got out in front of me, and instead of going with him, I tried to catch a hold of him. There was nothing in it really, I don't even know how the ref spotted it. That was their equaliser.

We gave them a few other chances, soft frees and the like, and it was gone. Instead of being left with a couple of weeks to prepare for an All-Ireland final, all you're left with is the what if. But that game – to come so close against the side who eventually went on to win the All-Ireland – it gave us the little bit of hunger, the sniff of success, and the reassurance that maybe we weren't as far away as people had once thought.

———

The Christmas after John got out of prison was the best I've ever seen him. The John I knew was either stick thin because he was on heroin, or blown up like a balloon because he was on methadone. Because he was taking drugs from such a young age, I had never seen him as an adult clean. And here he was, walking in the front door, and he just looked healthy. I nearly didn't recognise my own brother. It was such a weird feeling.

Prison had forced him to get clean. Even in a place as tight as Belmarsh, inmates would always find ways to get drugs onto the wings, but if you were pulled for a drug test and anything showed up, you could say goodbye to your next bail application.

The drug treatment programme he was on in prison was a lot more severe than anything he'd been on outside. The prison doctor was medicating him, giving him phy, but the programme doesn't run indefinitely. Initially they want to give you enough to stop you from using heroin or anything else that you might get your hands on in there, to start you on a recovery path, but they cut you out quickly then and you have to come down off it.

John started to suffer from psychosis. 'There's voices in here in the cell with me,' he told Mam.

She tried to explain to him that his whole body was coming off drugs and it was just his mind playing tricks on him. It must have been brutal, being in prison and then having to go through the hell of withdrawal as well, but when he got home eventually, clean, he was like a new man. You start to think that you've turned a corner.

That might have been the year that he brought Debbie home to meet us.

We knew that John had a long-term girlfriend over in London. Her name was Lil, and they had met when he first moved over to live there. They were going out for a good few years, all throughout the time that he was in prison, and when he was released, he went back to live with Lil in her place.

The story about how he ended up meeting Debbie was probably one of those where there was John's version of events and then a slightly different, true version. The way he told it, there was a bit of trouble and John ended up with a bloody head and a bit of some lad's tooth stuck in it. Whether your man had given John a tooth to the head, or John had given him a head to the tooth, you wouldn't know. Either way, Debbie was there. She was a friend of one of Lil's friends, and she was the one who looked after him. John's head was gushing but she was able to wrap a towel around it and stop the bleeding for long enough to get him home to her house and get him cleaned up.

However it happened, there was a fight between Lil and Debbie soon afterwards, and John ended up leaving Lil and moving in with Debbie, and for a couple of years, he was very happy. It wasn't always an easy relationship, for either of them, but they both felt that they had found love.

Debbie was a Londoner, a nice girl, but life had thrown her enough anxieties and demons of her own to fill her days. She had a tough childhood, and while she wasn't dabbling in heroin in the same way that John had been, she struggled with tablets. She had a young son from a previous relationship and there were still a few loose ends with her ex that had never been properly tied up and caused her some trouble.

John always had women in his life, but never too many serious girlfriends, and even before he brought Debbie and her son home to meet us that Christmas, we knew she was special to him. There was a little hint of the happiness that the drugs had stolen. An awful lot of people couldn't relate to what John was going through, no matter how hard they tried, because it just wasn't part of their world, but Debbie got him, and even the fact of being in a relationship with her gave him the promise of a brighter future. We hoped it could be another part of the jigsaw when it came to him staying clean.

They got engaged, but they were never married. Debbie started to get a bit deeper into drugs, and when John found out she was sinking, he had to distance himself from her for his own sake, and they broke up. They lost the flat that they were in together and John went to stay with one of Debbie's friends while Debbie was living in a women's hostel. They were still seeing each other – together but not together, that kind of way.

John was with Debbie on the day she died. They had seen each other earlier that evening. They said goodnight, and when John turned to go home, Debbie went the other way.

He had made her promise that she would go straight back to her hostel, but she didn't. She met somebody along the way and that person gave her heroin. Debbie took an overdose and it killed her.

I never really spoke to John about losing Debbie. I didn't know where to start, and when it came to any of the problems in his life, he much preferred to keep those emotions to himself, buried.

But he didn't need to say a word for me to know that he was heartbroken. Every time he found a route through the maze, every time he felt that there might be some way out, the walls closed in again and smothered him just as quickly. We were always there for him, but as long as he was in London, the letters and the phone calls and the few days he spent at home, once a year, were his only bridge back to us. Debbie was immediate and she was every day. She was love, and something to live for.

To be engaged and then to break up with her, to surrender the only good thing in his life and push her away so that he could try to save himself must have been impossible, must have taken a strength that I don't think I'll ever be able to fully appreciate. Being with her that night, there, but totally powerless to stop the tragedy that was hidden a few hours away was the cruellest of all.

That pain was probably what pushed John to start using heroin again himself.

Mam and Lindy flew over to the funeral to be with him, and they could see he was in a bad way. They were waiting in the crematorium and John said to Mam, 'Do you know something, Mam? If anything ever happens to me, don't leave me here, sure you won't?'

That got Mam worried immediately.

'John, there's nothing going to happen to you,' she said to him. 'Why are you even saying that?'

But for whatever reason, he was insistent.

'Mam, if anything ever happens to me, don't leave me in England.'

And she said to him, 'No, I won't. I promise you.'

———

L ondon must never have seemed further from home to John than it did in September 2011. It will remain one of the great days in Dublin football history – to come from four points down in the last 10 minutes of the All-Ireland final, to win a first championship in 16 years with what was effectively the last kick of the game, and to do it against our fierce rivals from Kerry.

But there will always be a part of that day that feels incomplete, because John wasn't there to see it happen.

That season couldn't have got off to a worse start for me. I've been very fortunate with injuries throughout my career, something that I never take for granted. I've had very few non-contact injuries – strains or sprains or tears – and the few I've had have rarely been serious enough to keep me out of a game.

But sometimes you're just unlucky and there's nothing you can do about it. I was named on the GPA Team of the Year in 2010 – not bad recognition for my first full season at senior level – but I spent the first few months of the following year explaining to people that I couldn't play because of a freak accident in the gym, where somebody had dropped a barbell on my foot and chipped a bone in my toe.

When I came back into the team for the final few rounds of the league campaign, we were flying. There were still a lot of young faces in the team, but we were harder and more experienced. We went unbeaten through the round robin before we played Cork in the final, a chance for us to really find out where we stood and a chance for us to win a rare league title.

We played them off the park for the first 40 minutes that day, led by eight points, and lost. When you lose a lead like that in a big game, some of the criticism can get quite personal. People start looking at you, barstool psychoanalysts asking questions about abstract qualities like courage and determination and commitment. Some players hear that negativity and like to use it as motivation and fuel for the fire; I prefer just to block it out altogether.

When I have a bad performance, I just want to go straight back out and play again to put it out of my mind. I didn't want to be sitting around for six weeks after losing the league final before we played our championship opener against Laois. It was a game that we were expected to win and we did, but it was very nearly the beginning and the end of my championship for that season.

I went to make what should have been a fairly routine clearance, but as I spun to hook the ball away, a blue jersey came out of nowhere and cleaned me out. John O'Loughlin was moving at serious pace and as he tried to block me down, his body carried through my right leg. The lower part of the leg went in and the middle part of it, around the knee, popped out.

I was left crumpled on the ground. James, our physio, sprinted in to check on me, fearing the worst, I'm sure. But I was already after missing so much football at the start of the season, there was no way I was going off in my first championship match because of a bit of a knock.

'Strap it up so I can get back out there,' I told him.

The adrenaline helped me to run it off and I played the rest of the game, but once we were done and I sat down to take the weight off it, I could feel the fluid that had already built up inside it. When I took the strapping off, the whole knee had swollen up. It didn't look good and the scan pretty much confirmed everything that we feared. I had fractured the inside of my knee – two of the bones had hit off each other with the force of the contact – and on top of that, I had a Grade 2 tear in my lateral ligament, which had overstretched when my knee bent out the wrong way. The prognosis wasn't definitive, but the general consensus from the doctors and from James was that I'd be doing well if I managed to kick a ball again that season.

Even from my limited experience, you learn a lot about yourself when you're out injured. It's a tough place to be. I'd had such a good season in 2010, really felt that I had proved my worth, and now it was the middle of the summer and I'd barely kicked a ball. It's frustrating, and rehab is a lonely process. You spend a lot of time inside your head. Even though you're still in and around the squad and doing little bits, there's only so much you can do. It's hard not to feel a bit sorry for yourself at times, but that's totally counterproductive. You have to realise that the team has to go on without you, and you don't want to be bringing that negative energy to the group.

You hear plenty of stories about careers that have been cut short by injury or ended at a young age, and the knock-on effects that can last long after you've hung up your boots and tried to move on with your life. I know I am very lucky compared to other lads. When my follow-up scans came back a few weeks before the All-Ireland quarter-final, the rehab had gone much better than anyone expected. I missed about two months.

———

Dublin 0–8 Donegal 0–6. They'll be talking about that one for a while.

The game had already settled into some sort of pattern by the time I got on. I had missed the rest of the Leinster championship with my knee injury, and although I was fit enough to be part of the squad when we beat Tyrone in the All-Ireland quarter-finals, I barely got two minutes off the bench at the very end of the game.

About 25 minutes into the semi-final, Rory O'Carroll took a bang on the side and had to come off with a hip injury. That forced management to bring me on, probably earlier than they had planned, and once I was in there, I felt I could bring something a little bit different. Donegal's game-plan was blindingly obvious. They had everyone behind the ball and it was slowing down our build-up and making it very difficult to put together good scoring chances. I just wanted to get on the ball and kick it. That wasn't the game-plan that we had discussed, but I felt that if we started moving it quicker, maybe we could penetrate them a bit quicker.

Half time was approaching and there had only been four scores, 0–2 apiece.

The hybrid defence was still in its infancy, and Donegal under Jim McGuinness were one of the first to really commit to it and take it to its extremes. The best way of describing it is like playing a game of five-a-side football. When you've got the ball, all of the opposing team will get behind it to try and suffocate the space you have to play in. If they manage to win it back, or when the lad on your team who thinks he's Ronaldo has a go from the edge of his own box, all of your team get behind the ball and try to do the exact same thing.

We had studied Donegal so we knew that they were going to play a defensive game. That was no surprise. But after those first few minutes, we realised that we were up against a much more extreme version of anything we could have expected.

We had a reputation for being a hard-working side that would shut down the opposition first and then look to build our own attacks, but this was a whole different animal. They had all of their players behind the ball. It seemed like a crazy way to play, but you could see what McGuinness was thinking – when you're defending, why not get everybody behind the ball and use everything that you've got at your disposal to stop the other team?

When you come up against that kind of tactical puzzle on the pitch, you have to embrace the challenge and adapt. You grow into a better player because of it, and the team evolves and becomes more versatile as well. Otherwise there's a very good chance that you'll end up playing into the trap that your opponents have set for you. Adapting doesn't mean playing the game on their terms either, but there's never going to be a one-size-fits-all game-plan that you can just roll out of the box every single time. Playing at the top level is all about developing game intelligence. If you train in such a way that you're used to thinking on your feet, then when you have to make a decision in the heat of the moment, it's smarter, quicker, and better than it would be otherwise. Even then, as players, we don't always make the right choices.

Donegal's problem against us that day was that when they had the ball, it was too hard to transition out of defence and into attack. Every time they turned us over, they were trying to carry it out from the back and run it up the field to try to create a score. For one thing, you'd be wrecked, no matter how good your conditioning is. Gaelic pitches are big enough fields – you wouldn't want your whole team to be running 100 metres up and down for 70 minutes. Their approach was a little bit more refined the next season and they went on and won the All-Ireland. It might not have been the prettiest thing to watch, but it worked.

If you told us before any game that we'd only concede six points, four from play, over 70 minutes, we'd expect to have a comfortable enough win, no matter who the opposition are.

We only scored eight, and four of those were frees, so it was anything but comfortable really.

But it was enough. We didn't need to kick down the door and take it off the hinges; we just needed to wedge it open far enough so that we had room to slip through.

———

Anybody who shared in the 2011 All-Ireland win with us – family, friends, fans – will treasure that day for a long time. That night after beating Kerry, we were in the Burlington at the official team banquet. All of the formalities were over, *The Sunday Game* cameras were packed away, and the party was really getting started. I rang Mossy and Cathal, another one of my closest friends growing up. The pair of them had gone off out to celebrate after the match.

'Where are yis? Come down to the Burlington to the after-party and have a few drinks down here with us.'

They were only delighted to be asked. They were getting ready to jump in a taxi and they rang Doc.

'We're going in to see Philly. They're all in there at the after-party. You coming?'

And Doc said, 'What's the dress code? All the team are going to be wearing their suits and all, won't they?'

I don't know if he had a suit ready or whatever, but later on that night, he showed up at the hotel wearing this suit that was, let's just say, a little bit tight on him. He was in such a panic that he'd gone in and taken one of his younger brother's suits. He was like a penguin, nearly busting the buttons on it, and the other two lads, Cathal and Mossy, hadn't even bothered getting changed. The pair of them had come straight in still wearing their Dublin jerseys. It was comical. Doc made a fairly quick exit in the end. I don't think he fancied putting up with the slagging for too much longer.

I didn't see John until a couple of months later, and he swore to me that he would never miss another one of those days again. He didn't think that he'd have to wait too long to come back to see us win another All-Ireland, but after the incredible high of 2011, 2012 brought a whole new challenge for us, one that we never really rose to. It felt like we never found our stride that summer, and all around us, the other teams were upping their standards. In those circumstances, it's very difficult to enjoy your football. I still don't have any definitive answers as to what went wrong. Was it down to our hunger? Were we underperforming? Were Mayo just a better side than us on the day that they beat us?

The All-Ireland semi-final was Pat's last game in charge. He had taken us to a new level and we had done something that hadn't been done for 16 years. Now I wanted to find out what we needed to change to take that next step, not just to win another All-Ireland, but to succeed where we'd fallen short that year. To defend it as well.

———

Mam drove down to North Wall to meet the ferry coming in. Five o'clock in the morning, still pitch black, and most of the city fast asleep in bed. Silent night, all was calm – and then as the boat got closer, she could hear John before she could see him.

'Ma! Howwwwwwaya Ma! Alright Ma!'

There he was, hanging over the deck of the boat, one hand

wrapped around a can and the other wrapped around the railings, roaring his head off. Locked.

Mam was sitting in the car, looking out the window at him and praying that he wouldn't fall in. He swayed his way down off the ship. The can in his hand obviously wasn't his first of the night, although he probably tried to blame his jelly legs on the rough crossing. God, it was good to be back. A big hug and a kiss for Mam and the two of them headed for home.

As soon as he jumped into the car, John knocked the radio off. He didn't want it or need it. He sang the whole way home – 'Driving Home for Christmas', of course. They pulled up outside the house and the blue lights Mam had attached to the railings lit the steps all the way up to the front door. She had spent days getting the house ready for him.

'They should be yellow ribbons tied around that, not blue lights,' she said to him and started to sing. The pair of them laughed. We didn't have any old oak trees either but John knew we still loved him, that was for sure.

He went into the spare room and there was a suitcase there full of brand new clothes for him. 'Don't bring any clothes home with you,' she'd warned him. 'I have everything you need here.'

Underneath the tree in the sitting room, there was a pile of presents, all neatly wrapped and labelled, one to each of us from John. Mam and Kellie had been working overtime in the shops before he came home.

Those few days were always special. We went down to Mam and Dad's on Christmas morning to unwrap the presents, and then the big dinner and a couple of drinks. Maybe a bit of karaoke later on that night. There's a video of John and Mam dancing in the front room, a photo of me and him, and he's wearing a T-shirt that says 'World Series Champions 2011: The Dubs'. It was simple, but it meant the world to have the whole family together again and forget about all of the other worries in our lives.

John loved being home with us, but it wasn't easy for him. He couldn't really leave the house. We certainly didn't want him going out, and he knew himself that once he stepped outside the front door, the only place he could go was back to the blocks to meet his old friends. He didn't need to be around drugs. He didn't need that sort of temptation.

We always felt that it would be much easier for him to stay in London and get clean than it would be for him to do it here at home. When he was at home, we felt that all it would take was one conversation with somebody that he connected with and he would be back on drugs. We were in a predicament. Mam especially wanted him home, but we thought if we brought him home, it would kill him, that he would be even worse than before and he wouldn't survive. We thought bringing him home was the worst thing we could do. But the fact is, no matter where he was, whether he got clean again or not was always going to be down to his decision.

After Debbie died, John was still living with her friend for a while and sleeping on the couch, but as it came close to Christmas, he had to move out. He got a hold of the key worker that he used to talk to the odd time, and he sorted him out with a place in a hostel in Hackney, the roughest, most run-down part of London.

John absolutely hated the place. He tried to explain it to us when he was home.

'You'd want to see the place that I'm living in now,' he said. 'There's cockroaches coming up out of the corner.'

We started slagging him and having a bit of a laugh – here we go again, John – real Boy Who Cried Wolf treatment. Nobody believed him.

'Stick newspapers down the pipe,' Dad said to him. 'They won't get through that.'

But John was adamant. 'I can't even eat the food there, Ma, it's sick.'

He went on. 'And do you see when someone dies? They're not found for days.'

'Why do you think that is?' she asked.

'I don't know if it's got to do with their DLA,' he said – the disability living allowance that they got from the government once a month. 'Maybe people aren't saying anything until the cheques come through and they're taking them.'

We told him to stop being so paranoid and exaggerating. There was no way the place would still be operating if it was as bad as he was making it out to be. It was, he insisted.

As I went to leave, I called John down to the front door to say goodbye to him, away from all of the others. I knew he was struggling for cash in London so I'd always slip him a few quid before he went back over, but the two of us were smart about it as well. We'd do it where Mam couldn't see us and she wouldn't know, and then John would go and get more money from her before he left. He'd never ask me for money, and there were times when he was too proud to take it and he'd make a show of brushing me off and telling me he was grand, but I'd still find a way to stick it in his bag or jacket pocket when he wasn't looking. I know he appreciated it.

He came down to the door, and I gave him a hug and pressed a €100 note into his hand. Enough to keep him going for a little while.

'I don't want to hear from you until you're off everything,' I said to him.

We said goodbye, and I headed for home.

———

Mam does this really annoying thing when she wants to talk to you on the phone. She rings, and if there's no answer, she rings again immediately. As if you might have magically become available in the space of those three and a half seconds.

If there's no answer again, she'll ring a third time. And probably a fourth.

Then she'll leave a message.

'Hi Philip, it's me, Mam. Ring me when you get this.'

Jesus, Mam, I know it's you. I've got caller ID. Your name flashes up on my phone when you ring me and there's 17 bleedin' missed calls there now.

It's usually the same story then when you eventually ring her back.

'Ah, I was just ringing to see if you're in work today and if you're calling up later.'

To put it simply, it's not unusual to have a heap of missed calls from Mam. You wouldn't think anything of it. And I didn't, even though this time she'd only tried to call me once, and there was a second missed call from my sister as well.

I was in the middle of a personal training session with a client, and the guy was there mid-rep. Not exactly ideal timing, for me or for him. I'd call them back afterwards.

A couple of minutes later, the phone started buzzing again. My sister again. I can't remember which one because that little detail is far less significant than the news she was ringing to give me.

I could hear the crying at the other end before she even managed to force the words out.

'Philip. Come home quick. John's dead.'

I walked straight out of the gym and got into my car and started driving. It's only five minutes from Ballymun Kickhams to Mam and Dad's, but when I came down off the

M50 roundabout towards Ballymun, I found myself doing a U-turn and driving straight back up to the club.

I walked back into the gym and the lad I was training was just getting his stuff and getting ready to leave.

'Right, let's go,' I said. I was ready to finish the session.

He obviously knew something was up.

'What happened, what's the story?' he asked me. 'Are you alright?'

'Yeah yeah, I'm grand,' I said, but I was in such total shock that I didn't know what I was saying.

It was the weirdest feeling I've ever had. Your brain is telling you not to believe it, that it didn't happen. If I just turn the car around, go back up, and carry on with what I was doing, everything will be alright. I actually thought it was déjà vu. I thought it was a dream that I'd had, and that this was just a déjà vu moment.

Have I been here before? Have I seen this before? But I hadn't ever heard or seen this.

My phone rang again. It was my sister.

'Where are you? Come down.'

I knew then that it was real.

I got back into the car and I drove. Fast enough. I got into the house and they were all there. I could hear everybody crying.

I opened the door into the sitting room where they were and I couldn't actually go in, so I shut the door and just ran upstairs.

I was in my room. Dad came up, sat down beside me on the bed, and gave me a hug.

# THE
# SECOND
# HALF

Young people are meant to be the life and soul of a community. The schemers and the dreamers.

That should have been John. That should have been so many others that we grew up with.

And it would have been, except drugs wiped out a generation and ripped the heart out of Ballymun.

At the funerals, there was no hiding from the fact that a young life that was still so full of promise and potential had been snatched away, just like that. There were moments that reminded you of how unique that life was, how special that person was to their family and friends, and they're the things that stay with you. Through bleary eyes, the funerals were such powerful statements of love and support and defiance, and at the same time, we felt powerless to stop this. Nobody escaped untouched. We went through so many of those days that we were left exhausted. Shattered.

The two worlds combine inside the church. Hundreds of mourners from around the area, a reminder of how much that person was loved and cared about, and beside them, row after row of zombies who were struggling with their own addiction. You look around and you think to yourself: how are any of these people going to get clean?

There are dealers everywhere, waiting to pounce on the first moment of weakness or opportunity. Parasites sniffing around, right there in the congregation, trying to deal at a funeral. The priest is there, trying to make sense of a tragedy, and the dealers are down at the back of the church, in people's ears.

'Are any of yis looking for zimmos? Yis looking for zimmos?'

That's how disgusting some people can be. That's how deep it is, how hard it is for drug addicts. What chance do they have if dealers are trying to smother them at funerals?

The day we buried John, one of his friends came over to me to give his condolences. John's friend looked well that day, like he was clean. We chatted for a few minutes.

'Do you see the hurt in this church today?' I said to him.

'Yeah, yeah.'

'Do you want your family to feel that?'

'No,' he said, as if it was the most obvious thing in the world.

'If you don't stop doing what you're doing, this is what you're going to do to your family.'

I wanted to shake him, to shout at him, to do whatever it took to make him realise. Not just him, but everyone in that church who was using drugs. For them to make that connection between the pain we were going through, and the love that they had for their own family.

But they're only words to someone wrapped up in addiction. The drugs bury that love.

———

All I could think about was not crying. I had it in my head that I had to be strong, for Mam, for my sisters, and being strong meant not crying. It's so stupid. Your big brother is lying there in a box a couple of feet away from you. He got 31 years on this planet, most of them a struggle, and that's it. All of those little moments that the two of you shared, that you took for granted, that's all you get. No more. No matter how hard you wish. That's what death is. There are no exceptions or second chances. It's brutal.

You'd give anything, everything, to have 10 more minutes. To go back and kick the ball around one more time, or to grab the £20 note from his hand and run down to buy the Kinder

Buenos. One last dinner, one last letter, one last phone call. Even for him to be back on the blocks, at the worst of his addiction, just so you could tell him one more time how much you love him, and for him to know that for as long as he is in this fight, you will never stop fighting alongside him.

There was so much I wanted to do with John once he got his shit together. I couldn't wait to get him into one of my gyms, get him trained up, and give him a job. His natural physique – that tall, lean, wiry frame – would have made for a great MMA fighter once he put the muscle back on and started training properly.

That was the plan, even if the weight of the coffin as it dug into my shoulder was one final reminder that John wasn't a gangly teenager any more, and that he would have had a long road to travel before he got anywhere near to that point.

We decided not to have a eulogy so that we could keep the ceremony as short as possible, and it was only when I stood up to lift the coffin that I realised how many people were in the church. Every seat was taken, all of the benches full, and the rest of the people were standing at the back of the church and all around the edges. I hadn't noticed.

'Fast Car', the Tracy Chapman song, started to play. That was it. All of the emotion that I'd been fighting against and bottling up came pouring out.

John's funeral was on 21 September 2012, a Friday morning, two weeks after he died. It had taken a while for the post-mortem, and for us to fly his body home from London, so we had plenty of time to tell people. In the blur, you pick out faces, and it might only be weeks or months later that you process that information and you appreciate what it meant to have them there.

Sitting on my bed, still numb and the reality that John was gone forever only starting to sink in, Mick was the first person

I had called. All of John's old friends were there. Teachers who had taught both him and me. All of my mates. All of the Dublin lads, the management, and representatives from the county board. There were so many people who wanted to be there to support me, you'd swear that it was my funeral as well.

We stepped out through the back door of the church and I caught Davey's eye standing outside. The whole team were there, all wearing their Ballymun Kickhams jerseys, lining the path on either side in a guard of honour for John. I'll remember that image, the two rows of red and green, forever.

———

The street was packed, full of crowds and crowds of people selling whatever they could from stalls, and immediately I felt uneasy. It was a lovely day, sun shining, but this felt like a part of the city that the rest of London had left behind. Shops closed down, forgotten buildings boarded up. In the evening, when all of these stalls were packed away, there would be nothing left. Something didn't feel right to me. It didn't feel like a place you could call home.

The three of us stepped out of the chaos and into the hostel where John had been living.

I hadn't slept much the night before. It was a few days since he had died, and me, June, Kellie and Mam had flown over to collect his things and bring his body home. We stayed out by the Olympic Stadium, where they were starting to pack up after the 2012 Games. It barely registered. Tossing and turning in bed, all of those different memories of John were running through my head.

He had tried to tell us that Christmas about the filthy conditions he was living in, but if any of us had known the reality, we would have insisted that he come home immediately. We would have found a way to make things work back in Dublin.

The staff showed the three of us up to his bedroom. There was nothing there. Small and bare, just a bed, a little fridge, and a bit of a telly. The rest of John's stuff, the bits and pieces of belongings that made up his life, had been taken away. I'll never forget the smell. I ran back outside and got sick.

The night he died, the only food in John's room was two slices of bread. And on the table, an envelope addressed to me. A birthday card.

———

John didn't die from an overdose, but after years of fighting against drugs, his body couldn't take any more. He died of an arrhythmia. His heart gave up.

We don't even know when he died: 7 September is the official date of his death, two days after my 25th birthday, but the best that the coroner could do in the post-mortem was to tell us that he had died some time between the 5th and the 7th.

There was a guy living in the hostel that John would have palled around with a little bit. He wasn't a friend, really, but a guy that he would have seen around the place and said hello to and maybe had a drink with the odd time. He said that he heard a loud shout late one night. That's as much as we know.

Mam had called him a few weeks before he died. She sat at the kitchen table with Dad and one of their friends and put him on loudspeaker. It was a little while after we had beaten Laois in the All-Ireland quarter-finals and they were chatting away about the match as well as some other stuff. John had been sick the week before that, badly run down, and he was after getting pneumonia. He wasn't quite right.

'I don't know what's wrong with me now, Ma. I've an awful pain in my hip and my leg is gone all numb.'

These are the bits and pieces of conversations that you can never quite put out of your mind. Mam brought it all up at John's inquest – the condition of the place he was living in, what he had said to her about people not being found for days after they died, and the fact that he'd been sick. The coroner assured her that all of John's vital organs had gone to St Thomas's and they had checked and that there were no signs of anything beyond the arrhythmia that had killed him. She couldn't shake the feeling that maybe he had a blood clot. She still can't.

———

In the station, the police officer handed me the envelope that they had found by John's bed.

'I take it you're his younger brother?' he said. 'He left you this. There were a few tears in eyes around here the other day.'

Folded up inside the birthday card was a letter, and in it, John told me one last time how proud he was to be my brother. When he couldn't come home for the All-Ireland final in 2011, he was devastated, and he promised me that he would never miss another one again. A couple of times that year, we discussed the plans for him to come back if we made it that far again in 2012. But we lost in the semi-final against Mayo, and a few days later, John died.

John wrote about how he wanted to move back home to us, to leave London behind him and find a way to rebuild his life with us by his side. But first he wanted to get clean again. Totally clean. He had stopped using heroin at that stage, but he wanted to go another step further, so he was going into rehabilitation that weekend to help ease himself off the methadone as well.

We don't know what forced him to that breaking point, what had finally made him see that he still had a choice, that there was a better way to live his life. Maybe he looked at that disgusting boxroom that was the closest thing he had to a home, and realised that he couldn't go on living like that. Maybe losing Debbie had given him the push he needed to get off drugs forever.

We never got a chance to ask him.

I didn't really speak about John's death or how it was affecting me. You get so much support from your family and friends and community at a time like that, and it's priceless, but I never wanted to talk to anybody. There was definitely a part of me that felt that very few people would understand what I was going through, that it would be very hard to have that conversation with somebody who hadn't lost a brother themselves. I don't think I was hiding from it, but my attitude was to just get on with things. Again, I was caught up in that idea that I needed to be the strong one for the rest of the family.

I dealt with my grief in the only way I knew how, by throwing myself headfirst into work. I never thought of it as a type of therapy, but definitely I was working so much, such long hours, that I didn't have time to think about losing John. It was only a few years later that I really started to confront those emotions and try to understand them.

Because John was living in London, the funeral was much more expensive than it would normally have been. We had never really been in this situation before and there were so many things that we had never thought of. We didn't have a family plot in a cemetery or anything like that, so we had to arrange to buy John's grave out in Dardistown. Little details, like the fact that we would need a bigger coffin because John's body was still so bloated from the methadone. We really wanted to have an open coffin, but we were worried that, because the post-mortem had taken so long, it wouldn't be possible. Thankfully, the funeral home did a great job of looking after John's body and it was.

Our friends and community pulled tight around us. A good friend of mine who works for Aer Lingus, Seán Murphy, rang me to offer his help in flying John's body home. Again, we didn't even know where to start, and Seán was a massive support to me and my family.

We wanted the funeral to be a celebration of John's life, and it was. The plan was to keep the ceremony short at the church and graveyard, and then have everybody back for food and drinks where we could tell stories about John and play the songs that he loved. I took on the job of organising the afters, but a couple of days before the funeral, I still had nothing sorted and I was starting to panic a little bit. I rang the chairman of Setanta GAA club, a man named Prionsias Ó Conghaile, to see if he'd be able to help us out and explained the situation to him.

'Prionsias, we're a bit stuck. Is there any chance we could use the bar in the club on Friday afternoon?'

He couldn't have been more accommodating.

'Of course, yeah, that's no bother,' he said. 'We'll look after the sandwiches for you, just come in whenever you're ready.'

I told him that wouldn't be necessary, that if we could have the room, I'd look after the food myself, but I was so taken aback by his generosity. I hadn't hurled for Setanta in years. A small club, and they went out of their way to help us and to make sure that we were looked after. The GAA and Ballymun, taking care of their own.

The party that we had to remember John the night of his funeral was amazing, the perfect celebration of his life and what he meant to all of us. I'll be grateful to Proinsias, and to Setanta, for what they did for our family for a long, long time.

All of those funeral expenses added up, and I had decided that I was going to pay for it all. That was my way of dealing with John's death. Obviously, Mam and Dad and my sisters were having none of it and they insisted that they all put their own bit in and we'd cover the costs between us.

Everyone helped out, but I was determined to pay for a chunk of it. I took a loan out of my business to cover the costs, and then I went and signed up as many personal training clients as I could manage. I was training 20 or 30 clients a week, spending about 60 or 70 hours driving between the three gyms in Ballymun, Drimnagh and Tallaght. I was leaving the house at six o'clock in the morning and not getting back until after 10 o'clock at night, absolutely exhausted by it. That was my whole life. It was so dangerous. I'd be on the M50 going from one client to the next, nearly nodding off in the car and starting to drift over towards the next lane before I snapped out of it. I was lucky nothing bad happened. In the space of two or three months, I made a lot of money to help pay for things, but I was ruined by it, so burnt out. It was horrible. I've never really liked training clients one-on-one since. But I needed to do it. I needed to keep myself busy, keep myself out of my head.

———

I'm not a very religious person. Like a lot of Irish people, I was raised a Catholic and I go to mass for christenings, funerals, and weddings, but that's about as far I go in terms of religion. For me, when a person dies, that's it. So I struggled the night before John's funeral, when we had his body back to Mam and Dad's place for a wake. He's there and yet he's not. You have to deal with that moment where you see a loved one in a coffin, no life in them, and the reality is that they don't exist any more. You're trying to say goodbye to them, to tell them how much you love them so that you can let go, but it's just a body. The person you loved is already gone.

John's dead and the harsh reality is that there's very little I can do to bring him back – not very little, there's nothing I can do. Every time I have to speak about him, every time his name is mentioned in passing, every time I see two brothers out having the craic, I'll think about him and, even if it's only for a second, I'll feel that same sadness and longing to have him in my life. That's human, and nobody is immune from it. But at the same time, there is a choice there, the choice to accept that loss as a part of who you are from that day onwards, but find the way to use it as a positive. Grief will drag you down if you let it, or it can give you energy. That's up to you.

In the years that followed, I came to realise that losing John was the half time talk of my life. It's a very simple way of thinking, but it's incredibly powerful. Half time in a match is so much more than an opportunity to get your breath back and rest the legs and get a bit of water on board. It is, fundamentally, a chance to regroup and reflect. All of the other stuff is secondary to that.

When you're sitting in the dressing room at half time, the first thing you have to accept is that you can no longer change anything that happened in that first half. It might have been good, it might have been bad – it doesn't matter, it's over. What you can do is think about it, learn from it, and use it to shape what you're going to do in the second half. There's no point in thinking that the rest of the match is predetermined, that you're locked into this fixed way of thinking or of playing because of what's happened in the first half. If sports teams went out thinking like that, imagine how many great comebacks we would have been denied over the years. Even if you've been brilliant in the first half, there's always room to be better when you go back out there.

Before John died, I thought I was living a good life, and in a lot of respects, I was. I was playing senior inter-county football and, more than that, I had won an All-Ireland. I had embraced education in a way that I never thought possible, gone back and repeated my Leaving Cert, and gone on to get a university degree. I had created a successful fitness business from the bottom up and owned three gyms.

But when I look back now, I can see that I was coasting through life. I didn't appreciate what I had, and how grateful I should be for it.

I was living a reactive life, rather than a proactive life, and so many people are making the exact same mistakes that I made, going through life on autopilot. Living from week to week, getting their wages and going out at the weekend, and then waking up on a Monday morning with a mind full of negative thoughts, already in a bad mood before they even get out of bed and start to get ready for work.

We don't take risks unless we have to. Life is a game, this is your half time, and you should be thinking, 'I'm going out to get man of the match in my life.' Don't be stuck in injury time when the ref is about to blow the final whistle on your days, thinking, 'I should have done this' or 'I should have done that.'

The problem is that too many people wait until something significant happens before they hit half time. An illness or a bereavement, or you split up with your girlfriend or boyfriend, or you get divorced. We won't lose weight or take our diet seriously until a doctor tells us that we're going to die.

John's death changed the way I looked at the world. It gave me a deeper understanding of what I was doing with my life, which in turn pushed me to strive for more.

I just wish I didn't have to lose him in order to make that change.

———

'Come on, Da, we'll get out of the house for a couple of hours.' He needed the distraction as much as I did. The two of us jumped into the car and drove up to watch the lads play. We stood on the line and tried to take our minds off everything else. Anyone who spotted us made a point of coming over, a quick handshake, how are yis getting on, let us know if you need anything. There was another game not long after that, when Kickhams played Crossmaglen in a challenge match. Again, I wasn't playing, but Aaron Kernan found me afterwards. The two of us have come up against each other a few times for Dublin and Armagh, and Aaron wanted to offer his condolences in person.

Funerals are hectic and it's only once that fuss settles down that the loneliness fully hits you and you realise the void that's now a part of your life. Without me ever needing to say a word, the club, and my teammates especially, rallied around to fill as much of the silence as they could. If John's death had affected me in any negative way, nobody would have batted an eyelid.

Off the pitch, when there was no training or matches to occupy my mind, I had my bad days, but when I was playing football, I was in a good place. John was still with me but as spiritual motivation, reminding me to go out and work harder and harder, and to enjoy it every time I had the chance to put on my boots. It felt like a lot of my teammates saw that and latched onto it themselves.

We had the Dublin championship in our sights that year. Dec Sheehan had done a great job of gelling the young lads and old during his time in charge, and when Paul Curran took over, the balance was right with a good mix of youth and experience, and we felt that our time had come. Twenty-seven years was long enough for anyone to wait.

We could have won the county title in Paul's first season in 2011. We had Brigid's beaten in the semi-final, a point up with a couple of seconds left, and then there was one of those crazy decisions that sometimes goes against you and there's nothing you can do about it. We were miles ahead at half time, and Brigid's did well to make a game of it in the second half, but it looked like we were going to stumble over the line. They launched their last chance towards the edge of the square and Davey was having none of it – straight up into the air, clean catch, I'll take that, thanks very much. Even better, he had the presence of mind not to hoof it straight back to them, on the off-chance that there was enough time left for one more last attack. He brought it out, and sold one of their lads with a beauty of a dummy handpass – and the ref blew him for overcarrying.

Sometimes there are borderline calls, and when you're out there on the pitch, you see them the way you want to see them, but to this day I'll tell you that Davey did not overcarry that ball. If you were going to do him for anything, maybe do him for the dummy handpass, but it wasn't even a change of hands. I couldn't believe it. The ref gave them a handy free, they stuck it over for the draw, and it went to extra time. We lost the plot completely then, Ted and Davey both got sent off, and they ended up beating us by six. Brigid's again – sickened doesn't even begin to describe it.

We arrived at the latter stages of the 2012 Dublin championship the next autumn in serious form, still unbeaten in the league and not fearing anybody, but the club had been through a difficult few months. That summer, Sean Andrews had passed away suddenly. There are a lot of really good people involved with Ballymun Kickhams, but then there are a handful who are truly priceless, who give their hearts and souls to the club they love, who give it life through their passion. Sean was one, and so was Tom O'Donohoe, our club chairman at that time; that incredible 2012/2013 season had only just come to an end when Tom died in April 2013.

Sean and Tom lived and breathed Ballymun Kickhams. No matter what time of day or night it was, you couldn't walk into the club without Sean grabbing you and nearly breaking the bones in your hand with a big firm handshake that you'd never forget. If it seemed like he was always there, it's because he was. Sean had been a great club chairman himself in his time, and one of the driving forces that really fought to rebuild the club's juvenile structure in the late 1990s and early 2000s, who made sure that kids like me had a team to play with. None of what came next, in the months after he died, would have been possible without him.

There was an emptiness in the club when he died, a sense, spoken and unspoken, that someone irreplaceable had been lost. Fiach – Sean's nephew, Val's son – was in the senior squad. When the championship came back around again, we spoke as a team about Sean and we spoke about John, reminding ourselves why that green and red jersey was more than just a shirt. When you tap into that emotion, there's a danger that it can overwhelm you, but we found inspiration in our sadness and twisted it into an opportunity. It energised us as a team, me most of all.

I took a few weeks off when John died, but it wasn't long before I was back in the thick of it. We beat Parnells, and then our old rivals St Vincent's in a tight battle, and we were too good for St Jude's in the semis. Crokes were the only team that could stop us now.

The final minutes before throw-in. I have my head down and I'm listening. I don't even see who speaks, Davey maybe, or Eoin Dolan. I hear the message though.

'When you're tired out there, when you're struggling and you feel that you have given it your all and you don't have anything else left in you, remember you have Sean and John there to support you.'

Let's go.

It's standing room only in Parnell Park. The county board wanted to play the county final on the bank holiday Monday under lights and they were right – the place is absolutely rammed. The parade starts and we follow the Artane Band, like a big day in Croker. Davey leads us. You'd go to war with Davey. Nothing to worry about there.

And then the ref throws in and we're off. Paul Mannion might be a kid, but he's a lethal forward, and we know Crokes are going to try get him on the ball as much as possible. Give it to him all you want – I won't be far away. Five seconds in and he bolts, sprinting out from the edge of the square into the space on the wing. I'm after him like a light. He gets the ball and shapes left and right, but I'm not buying it, not a chance.

There's nowhere to go, no other option but to turn back and play it inside. I go after it anyway, like a dog. We're all like dogs. Every last ball.

We're all over them in the first few minutes. One of their lads stretches to try to cut out a pass and misses. Dean's in. He pops it to Ted and Ted knows exactly what to do, flicking it back into the space to where Dean has continued his run. He's blocked just as he gets his shot away, but puts the rebound over anyway. Less than three minutes on the clock – a goal there would have been some start.

The lads never stop moving up front, dragging their markers across every inch of the pitch. Jay's screaming at me – 'Look at the space!' – and I ping the ball 50 yards. He turns his man and tries to drop it into Dean. It breaks. Ted's there. He goes round the defender and has a go. The keeper is beaten, but it clips the top of the crossbar and goes over for a point. Ted's hands go straight to his head – how did that not go in? We're knocking on the door.

Mannion gets a yard on me and kicks a point to get them on the scoreboard, but they're getting nothing cheap, and we're looking dangerous. Trigger picks out Dean with a brilliant pass from inside our own half, and by the time he's on it, I've bombed forward and made the run off his shoulder. I've two lads inside, but the goal is there for me. I pick my spot in the bottom corner and put my foot through it. Too many bodies in the way. It comes off a leg and bounces clear.

We're first to the loose ball, Crokes not too far behind. Once we've got it back, I make my mind up to stay close to goal. Shane Forde is there too. Kev Leahy drops a high one in on top of us, and Fordey gets a fist to it ahead of the keeper. Goal! Eight minutes in, and we're winning 1–2 to 0–1. On another day it would be 3–0 to 0–1, but we'll take it.

They're straight down on top of us. Mannion gets away again, but the angle is tough. He scores anyway. We're cutting through them though and getting our scores, and Dean kicks a point that puts us six up. We can't afford to take our foot off though. I take a quick kickout from Curryier and try to move it on to Trigger, who has dropped back to get it. I leave him short and he's beaten to it. Easy score for them, and our lead is down to four again. Crokes don't need that kind of help, but they'll take it if it's going.

We finish the half well and get in six points up. More importantly, it's a fair reflection of how the game has gone in that first 30 minutes. Only halfway there though and nobody needs to remind us of that. Brigid's were eight up at half time in the semis the previous week and Crokes ended up winning that by six. They're bound to get a run on us for a few minutes, and when they do, we need to keep the head.

It starts to happen pretty much straight away. Score. Score. Score. Score. All from the same lad, their corner-forward, Pat Burke. He's on fire, we're on our heels, and the next score is a huge one. Dean gets it. Three-point game again, 1–9 to 0–9, and about 15 minutes left to play.

Crokes score again, pushing more players forward to see if we'll crack, but we won't. We've waited for this for too long to let it slip now. Jay kicks a point, then kicks another, turning to the Ballymun fans over on the terrace with his finger raised in celebration. They've given us their best shot but we're still three up – four up now, as Dean curls over another.

Concentrate on the process. That's the only thing that you can control right now. Easier said than done. For as long as we can remember, Kickhams don't even get to county finals, never mind win championships. There's two minutes on the clock, plus whatever extra the ref decides to add, and we're in very unfamiliar territory. As each of Jay and Dean's scores drop over the bar, the roar grows louder. Even if your mind wants to go there, you don't have time to think about what it would mean. All of the sacrifices made by families and friends and people who were strangers to you once upon a time. Everything that we have worked so hard to build together. It's all there on your chest anyway, stitched into the crest.

Mark Vaughan is on for Crokes, barely looking back over his shoulder before he kicks a point that he has no right to from out underneath the stand. We give away a free and he points that as well. Only two in it now, and all the noise is coming from their fans while ours look at watches and bite nails and do whatever it is fans do when you've waited for 27 years.

Crokes win the next kickout and the purple floods towards us. Every mile we ran in training, every hour we spent in the gym, we need it to pay off now, our lungs to fill that little bit faster than theirs, our muscles to hurt that little bit less. A goal would win it for them, but we've thrown up a wall in front of Curryier, tired bodies dragging themselves into harm's way to a place where they can shield him. No way through. We force the attack wide and Crokes take their point.

And then it's over, and every other emotion is replaced in an instant by pure disbelief.

Ballymun Kickhams 1–12 Kilmacud Crokes 0–14.

Jesus. We've done it. We've done it.

Lads are running and jumping and hugging and shouting and grabbing a hold of whoever they can. Others are on their knees. And in those first few minutes, as people pile out of the stands and onto the pitch to be a part of the moment, it hits you.

The journey. This team that was fighting relegation only a couple of years ago. Champions of Dublin.

Paddy is there, 17, 18 years after he first saw me and decided he could make me into a footballer. Make all of us into footballers. Champions of Dublin.

Ballymun Kickhams. The scumbags. The knackers from the flats. Champions of Dublin.

'GO ON, GO ON, GO ON THE BALLYMUN, GO ON, GO ON, GO ON THE BALLYMUN.'

Davey takes the mic to make his speech. First thing he does is thank Crokes. They've always been a team that we've looked up to, he says, and he's right. A great club, and this group in particular are a great bunch of lads. Class acts. They were the county kings for long enough, and they won an All-Ireland too, but this is our night and they couldn't be more gracious in defeat. There's a way to win and a way to lose and later that night we'll all go for a few drinks together, the way it should be.

Davey says his thank yous to Paul and to his backroom team, to Ken and Joe and Gerry and Tommy and Anto and Louise, and before he finishes up, he remembers Sean and the people that can't be here with us to celebrate. Ted is standing beside me, the cup in one hand, and he puts his arm around me when Davey mentions John. No words necessary. I know he'd be as proud as anyone.

———

That night, we celebrated like a club that hadn't won a championship in 27 years. That was the ultimate prize for us, the holy grail, but we didn't have long to savour it. I'm sure there were a couple of lads slow enough to get out of bed on Tuesday morning, but by Thursday night we were all back in training. The party was over and we had our sights set on bigger and better things. Other teams had come and gone before us and been the best in the county, but no Ballymun side had ever been the best in the province. The club had only ever played in one Leinster final, back in 1982, and they lost that day to Portlaoise. We had already matched the great teams of the 1980s, and now we had a chance to break new ground and make our own bit of history.

We believed. Dublin club football was as healthy as ever and whoever came through that ferociously competitive championship and went on to represent the county could be confident that they held a strong hand. We felt we were getting better with each game as well, rising to each new challenge as the battle raged around us. Thirteen days after beating Crokes, we were back out for a Leinster quarter-final and a trip to face Mullingar Shamrocks in Mullingar. We were fresh and we were buzzing. Davey got an early goal and we never looked back. A 12-point win.

More than any individual game or moment, the thing that stands out the most from that Leinster campaign is how much it brought us together as a club. Rainy, windy days in November and December aren't ideal for football, or for fans, but with each game, the travelling Ballymun army got bigger and bigger. Cars and vans and minibuses hit the motorway in convoy. Country towns humming with the sound of Dublin's northside. Away grounds taken over.

There is no club without these people, the ones who cut the grass and the ones who sweep out the dressing rooms, the ones who are there to mark pitches and put up nets. Parents who give up whole Saturdays to bring their five-year-olds and six-year-olds down to football nurseries and, as they get older, ferry them around the city in threes and fours to matches. Auld lads who were there in '82 and '85 and waited patiently in the hope that they'd see those days again. They were all there. And it wasn't just the number of fans, it was their passion. I've never seen anything like the colour and chants that they brought to every game, the love of their club and the pride in their community. We were Ballymun and we wanted everyone to know it. Long after they had packed up and headed for home, the stands still echoed with their proud rallying cry: 'Go On The Ballymun'.

The semi-final was in Newbridge, a brutal day, the ball slipping and sliding in the rain against Sarsfields. It was a strange game. You work so hard for your chances in conditions like that, you have to make sure that you take them. Thankfully we did, and we didn't give their forwards too many easy scores at our end. Ted got a goal and that was enough to see us home. We won 1–8 to 0–5 – an ugly win, but a win nonetheless.

Portlaoise won the other semi and so, by coincidence, it's us and them again, 30 years after they had beaten us in our only Leinster final. We're behind enemy lines, playing them on their own patch in O'Moore Park. The second Sunday in December and there's Daz, one of the lads from the club, strolling through the stand dressed as Santa Claus, a cigarette hanging out of his mouth. He might have been a few weeks early for Christmas, but with that big red suit on him there's no question that Santa is a Ballymun fan. A win today would be the best present of all.

The weather is nowhere near as bad as the last day; still, nobody needs to be reminded that this is winter football we're playing. They get the first score, but we sort out our shape at the back pretty quickly. Everyone knows what's expected of them. All of the football is being played in our half, but we know we can soak up the pressure. When they shoot, we're on top of them. If they look to pass, we're in the way.

We go in ahead, 0–6 to 0–2, even though we've only scored once from play ourselves. Thirty minutes left, the last 30 minutes of a long year. After every game, people have been telling us about how fit we look, and it's true, we've put in the hard yards. But when you've got a group of lads that are playing for each other, fitness happens as second nature. We're young, we're buzzing, we're playing good football, we understand each other – fitness is a by-product. It comes easy.

Jay scores and we go six points up. We're well used to being in this position, and we'll be in it again before our season is over. In general, when you've built up a lead and the other team comes back at you and starts chipping away, the tendency is to start questioning yourself. Why did we stop doing what worked? But usually that's not the case. What's changed is that the other team is copping on and slowly solving the puzzle until they work out what they need to be doing better. And if you don't keep upping your own standards in each phase of the game or each half, they can get a foothold.

Maybe that's what starts to happen. Portlaoise get on top and they kick the next three points. They get brave – they've no other option – and start committing extra numbers forward. We can't keep the ball for long enough to build an attack of our own, but we're not panicking. We have our system, and they don't know how to break us down. They're getting shots away, but none of them are going over.

The clock hits 60 and Dean kicks his final free of the day. We're four in front and they need a miracle, which we'll never allow them to get. There are no nerves, only the limitless energy of the kids in Poppintree Park who would stay out there all night kicking balls if you let them. If others told us it was impossible, we never believed it. We've already proved that we're the best in Dublin, but this is bigger again. Our moment, our message to anyone who ever heard the word 'Ballymun' and swallowed the stereotype without giving it a second thought. For the first time ever, we are the champions of Leinster.

We go up into the stand to get our medals. Davey must be getting used to making speeches at this stage, but when he lifts the cup, he looks around, the cup in one hand, one of the handles in the other. We only have the thing a few seconds and we've already broken it. It must have been loose. Pass it along the line, but for fuck's sake, don't lose the handle. We'll never live it down.

Back in the changing rooms and the party is kicking off, lads half-dressed, either on their way into or out of the showers, but stopping to join in whatever chant has started up. John Small arrives in and rolls a shopping trolley into the middle of the floor. Boxes of Bud and Bulmers.

'Anyone for a can, lads?'

While the rest of us were getting changed, Smally had wandered off to the supermarket around the corner by himself, bought a load of gargle, and wheeled it back to us. A mad man. Before we leave, I jump into the trolley for a photo, hanging on to the cup by its one good handle and a smile spread across my face.

We haven't even got out of Portlaoise and we're already getting questions about our chances of winning the All-Ireland. We're the last name into the hat. Crossmaglen, going for three in a row, and St Brigid's of Roscommon are already there. Provided they don't slip up against the London champions, Dr Crokes will be there too. Nobody will give us a chance but we don't give a shit. We know it's likely to be us against Crokes in the semis, but that's in February, and this is December, and we're going to enjoy it for tonight.

———

Christmas comes and goes quicker than you think when there's an All-Ireland club semi-final on the horizon, and we were back in early January. Officially we'd been given a few weeks off to step away from football, spend time with our families, and recharge the batteries, but some lads could barely sit still for fear that they'd go stale.

I wanted to get a game under my belt. We managed to keep it quiet, but all throughout that Dublin and Leinster campaign, I had been playing with a bad rib injury. It happened early on against St Vincent's in the Dublin quarter-finals and was one of those unlucky ones. Two of us went up for a ball, and whatever way their lad jumped, his knee came through and caught me. I got up and I played the full game, not realising my rib was actually broken until I got it checked out afterwards. We were due out against Jude's the following week in the semis and I only had one concern: was I OK to play? Once I got the green light, there was never any question of me sitting it out.

I got through most of that Dublin and Leinster run without too much trouble, but I must have got a knock on it somewhere along the way because it flared up again and was giving me a bit of trouble. We had a game against Parnells in their place and I asked Paul if I could have a run to get a bit of fitness in. Instead of going in at full-back, where I'd usually play, I started in midfield and played really well.

Whatever I did, it obviously triggered something with Paul because he decided to change things around for the semi-final against Crokes. Davey moved into the half-forward line and I played in midfield with James. Sean George was flying in training and he came in at full-back to pick up Colm Cooper. We hadn't conceded a goal in our last four games, since the Dublin semi-final against Jude's, so it was a brave call, but I was delighted. Pushing me out the field was giving me the freedom to go and play. I want to be on the ball as much as possible, give and get and give, and the further up the pitch I am, the more I can do for the team.

All-Ireland semi-final day came and we arrived into Thurles. There were only a couple of thousand fans there, but it felt like they had bought every train ticket out of Dublin that morning – Ballymun on tour, our very own Trip to Tipp. A Saturday afternoon and the town centre was hopping. That carnival atmosphere carried on into the stands and there was a moment when I was there warming up on this beautiful, big, wide open pitch on the biggest day of my club career and part of me would still rather be up there with them, for no reason other than to share in the occasion. My mate Joycey is there, wearing this massive Teletubbies costume – the green one, whichever that is – and a Kickhams jersey over it. There's always one.

The bookies and a lot of the neutrals gave Crokes the edge. They were the ones with the experience and the reputation. We were absolutely rabid though, and none of them could have anticipated the intensity that we brought to our game that day. It was 10 weeks since we had beaten Portlaoise and we played like a team that had been locked up and starved of football ever since. Hubby was immense, and Georgey was like glue on Cooper. If there was ever any threat of him getting loose, we always had another man or two never too far away.

There's one moment towards the end of the first half that always stands out. Georgey is there, standing Cooper up, then Karl arrives in, and then Davey, suffocating him until he tries to wriggle free and, in doing so, overcarries the ball and gives away a free. Davey is screaming his head off. A war cry. We'll do this all day if that's what it takes.

I was in the thick of things at the start of the second half. In the space of 10 minutes I was booked, gave away a penalty, was blessed not to be shown a second yellow card and sent off, and then kicked a point. To be perfectly honest, I don't really remember all that much of it. Curryier saved the penalty, which was a massive let-off for us at a time when the game was still in the balance, so maybe that negative has been overtaken in my memory by all of the positives I associate with that day.

My point put us six up, and by this stage, we were starting to get used to our opponents having a purple patch, so when Crokes kicked four in a row without reply, some teams might have got a little nervy, but we held it together.

Ballymun Kickhams 1–10 Dr Crokes 0–9.

While that was still sinking in, we got word that there had been a shock in the other semi earlier that afternoon. Brigid's had beaten Crossmaglen. We wouldn't have feared Cross in the slightest, but they were out. It would be us against Brigid's, going head-to-head for the All-Ireland club championship in Croke Park on St Patrick's Day.

———

The Ballymun that I knew and loved as a kid is gone. It vanished with the last of the flats a few years ago. The regeneration scheme brought some good to the area, but it also did away with the heart of the old community. Places like the shopping centre, which for all its ills was a focal point for people, were shut down and left as empty shells, with nothing ever built to replace them.

Growing up, I was used to seeing Ballymun turn green, white, and orange when Ireland qualified for the World Cup, but I had never seen it turn green and red like it did in the fortnight before the All-Ireland club final in 2013. It's the most incredible sight, to drive up the Ballymun Road with the bunting and flags lining both sides of the road, and to know that it's all there because of something your team has done. It's a really special moment. It brings back a sense of community, belonging, and pride that has been fading away in Ballymun. Our home, the place that the majority of people have never given a chance, could potentially be the best club in the country. Maybe fairytales do happen in real life.

Journalists and TV cameras come, except this time they aren't there to write about drugs or overdoses or arrests or murders. They're ready to look beneath the label, find out who we are as a club, and tell people our story. We aren't the gang of lads from the towers that so many had presumed over the years. There are lads like me who lived in the flats, but there are also lads who live in houses in the estates, lads from Glasnevin, and lads from even further afield – Karl Connolly from Swords, Dean Rock who started out in Ashbourne, and James Burke who came all the way from Mayo. A mix of individuals and backgrounds and experiences, but one club, patiently rebuilt over the years around a team of talented youngsters. A club that never stopped being proud of the name Ballymun.

If we thought we had seen our supporters at their best up to that point, we hadn't seen anything like it, but you can't afford to get ahead of yourself and think about what it would be like to win and what it would it mean, for you or for them. There are kids on the streets and they're not wearing Man United or Liverpool jerseys any more – they're wearing Kickhams jerseys. You can't avoid the buzz. Everyone wants to wish you luck. Everyone wants to tell you how well you've done so far. Everyone wants to tell you how proud they are.

It's still hard to fully appreciate how well those opening 10 minutes went for us. We decided to change things up again and Paul wanted me to go straight in at full-forward, throw a curveball early on and see how Brigid's react. I don't have the first clue about gambling, wouldn't know my way into or out of a bookies, but because everyone was expecting me to be playing at full-back I was 60/1, or something like that, to be the first goalscorer. It didn't quite come off for anyone who had backed me – the game had only started and Dean got our first goal – but a couple of minutes later I scored our second. Dean kicked a free, James Burke popped up with a point and with only 10 minutes gone we were winning 2–3 to 0–1.

Senan Kilbride got a goal back for them quickly and he was having a little bit too much influence for our liking. The element of surprise of having me in at full-forward had worn off and I started to drift. I went out to midfield, dropped back to give Sean George a bit more cover and sweep, then I went out to centre-back before half time. When we came back out for the second half, I started at centre-forward, so in the space of 60 minutes I played in every line of the pitch that day, apart from in goal.

By half time, they'd cut our eight-point lead to four, and they clawed back the rest of the gap early in the second half. Eventually I switched in to mark Kilbride, who was doing most of the serious damage. There was also an awful lot of good ball going into him and that's hardly Georgey's fault, but by the time we made the change, it was too late. Brigid's were already on top.

When you lose a game as massive as that by one point in injury time, you're always going ask questions afterwards. Did we panic? Yeah. Did we have enough experience and maturity to see out the game from a strong position? Obviously not.

I had no idea how long was left when Frankie Dolan kicked that last point for them. I sprinted to the halfway line and Sean

Currie hit me with the kickout. As soon as I had the ball in my hands, the ref blew the final whistle. I turned and, out of sheer frustration, walloped the ball in his direction. I was lucky I missed by a mile and, as I kicked it, my whole hamstring cramped and I dropped to the ground. I couldn't even shake hands with the Brigid's lads or console our own fellas because I was lying on the ground for ages trying to get my hamstring stretched.

The anger gives way to sadness and hurt. Regret. You think about the 'what ifs'. You think about your club and your team-mates, your community and your family. It's impossible not to feel like you've let them down, even if you've already brought them further than they ever dared to dream.

It's only 60 minutes on the pitch, but it's a culmination of everything we've done since the first day Paddy pulled us out of that classroom to tell us what time training was at. To go on that adventure for the best part of a year, to do so many things that people thought you couldn't, and then come so close to winning the biggest prize of them all only to be beaten with the final kick of the game, it's hard to take. When you win on those big days in Croker, you always want to pick out the faces in the crowd; when you lose, you try not to look for fear of who you might see.

I used to be a really bad loser, but as time went on and I matured, I started to understand that there's no way you're going to play the sport and never lose matches. It's reality and if you try to fight reality, you're going to lose all the time. You have to take the good lessons that are there to be learned and try not to carry around the negatives that will eventually drag you back.

When we took a step back, we knew we had achieved something remarkable for our club, even if true greatness lay just out of our reach. Maybe the legacy of that season won't become obvious until a few years from now. We'll have more opportunities to get back to that stage as a team, even if we haven't quite managed it yet, and if not us, maybe the kids that saw that team play and were inspired to pick up a ball and join their local club, maybe they'll be able to stand on our shoulders and reach that little bit higher.

I finally managed to get back to my feet. We huddled in the middle of the pitch, gutted, as the party went on somewhere else without us. Extras in someone else's Hollywood ending.

In those few minutes, when the emotions were too painful to even consider, it felt like a day that could make or break a team. But if Ballymun means anything, it means fighting on when others would give up. I remembered the guard of honour lining the path outside the Church of the Holy Spirit, and the power that they had given me when I needed them the most. They had carried me through the toughest seven months of my life. Now I had to try to lift them.

I had something I needed to say.

'Lads, this is going to be a tough one for all of us. It has been a tough year for me too since John died, but in the last few months, I know that I lost one brother, but I gained 26 other ones.'

Red eyes met mine.

'This isn't the end for us,' I said. 'We'll be back.'

We'll be back.

———

Then I hit a wall. The early years of building up the gym business had been a rollercoaster, a really fast one where any feeling of control that I had was my mind playing tricks on me. Now I was at the part a split-second after you get to the top of the biggest climb and start that freefall, where your stomach rises up into your mouth and all you can do is panic.

In the months after John died, I started seeing problems everywhere. Ireland had come through the worst years of the recession, and for the first time in a long time, businesses were starting up rather than shutting down. The only problem for me was that every second new business seemed to be a gym or fitness fad or social media craze that was promising its clients the world and nibbling away at my revenue. The market in Dublin was totally saturated, with no regulation and no quality control, and that wasn't good for anyone, except for the cowboys whose only priority was a quick few quid. You could sign up to do a fitness certificate that took three months, or half a year at most, hang it on the wall and that was all you needed to set up your own gym. It's no surprise that they were popping up quicker than Starbucks.

I felt like the fitness industry was closing in on top of me, and I couldn't work out my next move. I looked at our balance sheets and the money we had made and convinced myself that the fitness and gym boom had hit its peak in Ireland. Things were tough, but the biggest obstacle to even more growth and improvement was one person: me.

Before John died, I might have thought I was a businessman, and told people I was a businessman, but I wasn't. In a short space of time, I had taken opportunities and built a business from nothing. That far surpassed any expectations that people had of me and, truthfully, any expectations that I had of myself starting out. The boy from Ballymun come good. It was easy to think that the hard work was done, that I had already made something of my life and built my empire, but I wasn't pushing myself. When I ran into problems, like a saturated market, I waited for solutions to come to me, and then looked for someone else to blame when they didn't.

When you're in your twenties, you might get up in the morning and go to bed at night and think that your whole life is still ahead of you, blank pages waiting to be written whenever you choose. But John only got a few scraps of paper, and losing him at such a young age forced me to realise that you can't expect to be successful any more than you can expect to live into your seventies and eighties. Life doesn't come with those types of guarantees.

Once I admitted to myself that I had been coasting along until John's death, that realisation gave me the buzz and energy to go and attack the business again. I was the one who had control over the business's success, not any of these external factors, so if I wanted the business to do well, I had to upskill and educate myself. I had to evolve myself to evolve the business. Up until that point, my business had really just been a job. From that moment on, it became my passion.

For the first time in my career, I went to a seminar. Thomas Plummer is probably one of the most successful consultants and speakers on the business of fitness, and as I sat there listening to him talk about different strategies, it was a complete eye-opener. It wasn't that the market was too crowded or that the business had lost its edge. We had so much potential. It was that I wasn't doing half of the stuff that I should be doing.

There's a quote that I love: 'The greater danger for most of us is not that our aim is too high and we miss it, but that it's too low and we hit it.' It gets attributed to Michelangelo, but the message is more important than whether or not he ever actually said it. When John died, I knew that I could take nothing for granted, and I completely transformed my business life. Instead of running a business that went into gyms in GAA clubs and managed them, I started looking at ways to compete against mainstream gyms and take a share of their market. Instead of panicking about the future and looking for a way to hedge my bets, I was thinking about bigger premises, what new systems I could introduce, how I got on with people, how I spoke to my staff, and how I could help them to develop.

I couldn't do it by myself. I remember the first time my business coaches Paul Fagan and Stephen Kirwan sat me down and asked me to go through my revenue figures.

'Let's start at the start, Philly. What was the number for last year, and what's the projection for this year?'

My face dropped. Not because the numbers were bad, or because I was embarrassed by them, but because I simply did not have a clue. I was running three gyms and I couldn't tell you how much money we took in last year, how much of it was profit, or what we were aiming for this year. That's how bad my business fundamentals were. Even on the basics – planning, punctuality, organisation – I was a disaster. I couldn't complete three tasks in a week, not because I was lazy or wasn't putting the time in, but because I didn't have a structure that would allow me to get things done. I needed someone to force that sort of accountability on me.

Once I realised that, I wasn't too stubborn or proud to go and ask for help. Podge Byrne was a friend and business partner of Pat Gilroy's when Pat was Dublin manager, and when I first met him towards the end of 2012, that was when I seriously started to grow and develop my businesses. Podge has been a great friend to me, a brilliant mentor, and one of the biggest influences on my business life. What started out as a quick chat to get a bit of advice turned into regular mentoring sessions, and he has invested a massive amount of his time into helping me to develop. Joe Dunne is another man who has given me a huge amount of help. Having people of their experience and success put that much faith in me gave me huge confidence to pursue my vision, and reassured me that I was going in the right direction.

I rebranded the gyms as Be.Do7 Fitness Club – 'Be Yourself, Do More, Become A 7' – the number seven being our shorthand for a member who has achieved their perfect balance of movement, strength, and body composition. The Fitness Club part of the name is important too: I want the people who have gone through all of these mainstream gyms, joined up, used the gym once or twice, and said, 'Aw I hate this,' and the people who might feel intimidated about going into a big gym to feel more comfortable coming in to Be.Do7.

At Be.Do7, the team is about a lot more than just training people. We're about getting people thinking more positively in life, because if we get people thinking more positively outside the gym, they come into the gym and they add energy. They get more results from that and we get more retention and more referrals and it's good for business. Our core belief is that if you can do 1% more every day, you become a better person – whether that's an improvement in your mindset, your activity, your nutrition, whatever it is: 1%, that's all we're looking for and if you can do that, you'll become a better person.

These people, the gym members, are one of the most important influences in my life. Every day when I go in to work, I have it in my head that I'm there to support somebody and to help somebody. I know all their stories. I'm like a family member to most of them. Some of them will come to me and tell me they're pregnant before they tell their boyfriends – which is a bit worrying – but they're that dedicated and determined that they'll want me to know why they're missing the gym.

For years I went to a gym and soaked in negativity because I wanted to listen to people's problems, hide from my own, and make myself feel better by comparison. Now what I'm trying to do with my members is to make them feel more positive. If they can feel more positive from what you're doing with them or teaching them or the tools that they use in the gym, in a way you're creating a little army there that reinforces positivity in your own life every day.

————

Over Christmas in 2016, I picked up a copy of Paul O'Connell's book and started to read. I was never much of a reader growing up, and now when I sit down with a book, I'm on the lookout for some hidden gem or insight that I can take and apply to my own life. I keep an ideas book, a little notepad where I can scribble down any interesting thoughts or concepts, and then I can refer back to it when I need to refresh my memory.

On the very first page, O'Connell talks about Munster's Heineken Cup semi-final in 2006 and how fit he felt towards the end of the game. He always looked back on that day as the moment when he was in the best shape of his life and chased that feeling, that benchmark, for the rest of his career. I wondered if he realised that at the time or only after the fact. I know that if I want to be in the best shape of my life, I have to think it as well as feel it. It's mental as well as physical.

When was that moment for me? What's the level that I've been aiming to get back to ever since? It was 2013, and nothing else even comes close. I still have a photo on my phone, top off and tensed, and in every muscle and sinew you can see how hard I was pushing myself in the gym at that time.

I had the time to do it that year, and I had the motivation. If you're lucky enough to be involved in a club campaign that lasts all the way to the All-Ireland final on St Patrick's Day, that becomes the number one priority and you won't be considered for the county panel until it is finished. By the time Ballymun's season was over, Dublin were a couple of months into their new league campaign, the first under Jim Gavin, and Jim's side had already started to settle into shape without me. I knew the door wasn't closed, that this was to be expected and I had to be patient, but I struggled to break in and win back my jersey.

I wasn't involved as much with Dublin, and myself and my girlfriend at the time had broken up, so all of a sudden, I had a massive amount of free time, the likes of which I hadn't seen in a few years. When I was younger and more insecure, I might easily have taken this to heart, a threat to my very existence as a Dublin player, but at 25, I knew I was about to hit my prime as an athlete and as a footballer, a very short window that would open and then be snapped shut forever just as quickly. I had to capitalise on it. I was in a position where other people's dreams were my reality, getting a shot that so many would love but so few actually get, and I couldn't be complacent about that or take it for granted. When it was all over, whenever that might be, I knew regrets about things I didn't do would haunt me more than anything else.

I saw being on the fringes of the Dublin panel as an opportunity, and went away to work on my own conditioning. I didn't have to be fresh because I wasn't starting any matches in the short term. The lads were playing well and performing well, so I had to wait until one of them, whoever was in my place, slipped up so I could get my shot. That's healthy competition within a panel, where you're all driving each other on. There was no way of knowing how long it might take for my chance to come, but I had to be ready, and I wanted to be in the best shape possible for when that happened.

I couldn't keep doing the same things and expect different results, and I quickly realised that my nutrition had been holding me back. In theory, I knew all of the right things to be doing. We had nutritionists coming in to talk us from a young age with Dublin, setting down the basic principles of what to eat and what not to eat, but I was a typical young lad. I got the piece of paper, stuck it in my bag, and never saw it again. You can get away with a lot when you're young. At that age, you can eat a bag of crisps and go out and play a game of football, and, provided you're not having a quarter-pounder and curry cheese chips and a bottle of Coke on top of it 20 minutes before you go out to play, you'll be grand. But once you start to get older and you start to understand the benefits of proper nutrition, it's only then that you buy into it.

I was exposed to some of the top nutritionists in the country during my time with the senior team, and from then on I was like a sponge with all of them, taking everything that they were telling me and trying to see what worked best for my body. I know now, for example, that genetically my body type is low-carbohydrate-sensitive, so if I eat a load of carbs, I will generally put on a lot of fat. I save the carbs for heavy training and match days and the rest of the time, my diet is paleo-based – lots of eggs and lean meat.

The science behind nutrition hasn't changed much over the years. The most important part is the compliancy, having the determination to take what you're being told to do and follow through with it. I had my own meal plan done out, was cooking for myself as much as possible, but I still couldn't stick to it because I was running a gym business and didn't have time. I realised that if I couldn't cook everything that I needed to be eating for myself, I had to stop making excuses and find someone who could cook it for me.

I asked around to see if anyone knew a chef that would be free to do some work, and I got set up. I was effectively my own nutritionist. I did all the calorie counting, worked out all the macros, and then passed him over the meal plan, and he cooked everything I needed for my daily allowance. I didn't want to be eating boring, bland food for breakfast, lunch, and dinner. I knew that I'd never stick to it. I wanted comfort food, the stuff that you'd normally only be allowed to have as a cheat meal. I had him make me healthy Thai green curries, shepherd's pie, burgers and chips, spice trays, Singapore noodles.

Within a couple of weeks my second business, FitFood, was born. I was an inter-county athlete and I was struggling to eat properly because my life was so busy, so it stood to reason that my members, or people in other gyms around the country, were under the same pressure. From working with my members, I could see the ultimate factor that was either helping them to get results or holding them back was their nutrition. Drawing up a meal plan, shopping, preparing a week's worth of food, and then cooking healthy meals are all things that take a lot of time. I wanted a business that would do all that for you, deliver it to your door, and then all you have to do is heat your food.

One of the biggest lessons I've learned, in business and in life, is to appreciate that you're on a journey, but not to presume you know the final destination. The way that FitFood has grown and developed as a business over the last four years is a prime example of that. When I started it in 2013, I started it as a home meal-delivery service and it took us over two years to develop that service properly. Now we've started to sell some of our meals through retail outlets and, ultimately, those sales will develop enough capital to allow us to open our first healthy food, grab-and-go type restaurant.

FitFood started from a setback – me losing my place in the Dublin squad – and my response to it – questioning the things that I could do to get to where I wanted to be, rather than kicking my heels and feeling sorry for myself. In times of adversity, I have always tried to double down and come back stronger. Maybe that's the Ballymun in me. After losing John, I learned to be so much more grateful for the many things that I do have, rather than the few that I don't. And if there's a twist in the road, follow it for long enough and you'll find an opportunity.

———

Trevor Croly was always good at spotting if something was bothering you, and he'd never be afraid to ask what was going on.

We had finished a session and the lads had all gone back inside to get changed. He wanted to know what was up.

'Walk across the pitch with me,' he said.

I've known Trevor for a while, and when he took over as Shamrock Rovers manager at the end of 2012, he was on the phone to me straight away. He wanted a strength and conditioning coach to come in and do a bit of screening with the squad during pre-season, to work out where there was room for improvement, and get the players moving in the right direction. I said yes.

We started walking and I explained to him about Dublin, how much work I was putting in, what great shape I felt I was in, and how I was struggling with the fact that after all that effort, I still wasn't getting a look in.

When we got to the centre circle, he stopped and turned to look at me.

'Right, we're only after walking halfway across this pitch,' he said. 'Do you know how many times you've said the word "I"?'

I hadn't a clue.

'Twenty or thirty times,' he said.

Point taken.

'All of these things that you're after explaining to me, the things that you're doing, are they what you are in the Dublin squad to do?'

'No,' I said.

'Look, it's simple,' he said. 'You need to find out what you're there to do. Find out what your job is with that Dublin team and stick to that. What you do with your club and what you do with your county are two different things.'

Playing for Ballymun, I was the lad in midfield that was getting on the ball, spraying it around the place to get attacks moving, pushing forward to get involved in attacks. Doing that when I was with Dublin was like trying to run before I could walk. I wasn't even in the team and I was showing up at training sessions and behaving like I was some sort of total footballer, and then looking around and wondering why I wasn't getting picked. There and then, my job was to be dogged, to be aggressive, to win my individual battle with the man I was marking. The conversation with Trevor made me realise that I was being selfish, and a little bit stupid too. It completely changed my attitude towards the situation and gave me a new focus when I was going training. From that point on, my objective was to do what I was down there to do.

Once I copped on a bit, I got my chance. I had come off the bench for the final 20 minutes of the quarter-final against Cork, but when the side was named for the semi-final against Kerry, I was back among the subs again. You wonder if that's how it's going to be for the rest of the year.

The reality is that GAA is a 26-man game, now more so than ever, and someone has to be the guy on the bench. From the time you're a kid, it is drilled into you in sport that no matter what number is on your back, you have to be switched on and ready because you never know when you're going to get your chance. That day against Kerry proved it.

When I came off the bench, there were only 17 minutes played, but at that stage we had already been two points up, then five points down, then back to all square. It was insane. By the time the full-time whistle went, people were already painting it as one of the most epic games of the modern era: two heavyweights going at it again in another chapter of their historic rivalry.

But once I got caught up in the action, the quality of what was going on barely registered. Kevin O'Brien had started at corner-back on James O'Donoghue and he wasn't playing to his standards. O'Donoghue had scored 1–2 early on and Jim and the management decided that they needed to change something. That's a big decision to make so early in such a crucial game and I have huge respect for them taking the risk and for trusting me with that opportunity. I'd like to think that I paid them back with my performance. I must have, because when Jim picked his team for the final, I was back in as the only change. What a time to be making your first start of the season.

For all that was special about our first All-Ireland in 2011, I felt that I had missed out on something. When you're a kid, you don't grow up dreaming of spending the biggest day sitting on the bench in the Hogan Stand, watching the clock and waiting and hoping that you'll get your chance before it's too late. For 46 minutes that day, that was all I could do, and because I was a sub, I never got a chance to walk in the pre-match parade. It might seem like a little thing to get hung up on, but it wasn't really about the parade. It was about what it represented – starting in an All-Ireland final – and it gave me something concrete to work towards.

When the team was named a few days before the 2013 final against Mayo and I was in the starting xv, I promised myself that I would soak it all in and savour every minute before throw-in. Even if you're focused, and even if there are nerves, it's still possible to do that. You have to enjoy it; you don't know when you'll be back again.

The number two jersey. I slotted in between Clucko and Rory O'Carroll. Looking up into the stands is such an incredible feeling. You pass little pockets where one set of fans outnumbers the other, but it makes no difference – the different chants and cheers all melt into one. And then you turn to face the Hill and make that long walk down the Cusack Stand side … and you can hear it.

'COME. ON. YOU. BOYS. IN. BLUE.'

The arms are all perfectly in sync, like they're trying to reach out and grab you and drag you up there with them. And as you get closer and closer, it gets louder and louder. I'll never know what it's like to be from another county and walk into that storm seconds before throw-in, but when you're a Dub, your heart would nearly come out through your jersey. That's the final part of the preparation done. Now you're ready.

I broke from the parade and jogged down to the Canal End to take up my position on Cillian O'Connor. Battle lines drawn. Within the first few minutes, I knew that I was sharp. The ball came across the edge of the square and he got there a split-second before me, the momentum taking the two of us into each other. We bounced apart, but when he turned to shoot, I was on my toes and right on top of him. I threw myself at the shot and got a block on it. Nine times out of 10, if you're not sharp, or you're not on your game, you're not making that block.

Then the adrenaline kicks in, and as the ball bounced clear, I was up and on it before he could get to it. I slid to the ground to scoop it up, half-expecting him to give me a nudge in the back and give away a free. He didn't and whatever way the ball bounced, I played it off the ground. The ref spotted it and blew for a free in. Fuck. After all that.

Making any mistake is bad. Making one like that that undoes all your hard work is twice as annoying. All you can do is put it out of your head and go again. Right, I told myself, you have a job to do today, and that job is to win your battle against O'Connor. Don't worry about anything else or anyone else. All I wanted was to keep him off the ball as much as I could and when he did get on the ball, keep him scoreless. If you can do that against a player of his calibre, that's a massive win for the team. It worked. He kicked a good few frees but he didn't score anything off me from play.

You're not going to give an inch in an All-Ireland final, and if that means putting your body on the line for the team, that's what it takes. Because if you won't do it, someone else will. That day in particular was like a warzone, men laid out all over the place. I got caught by a flying elbow underneath my eye and the whole eye swelled out. I went over to the line so that the medical team could look at it. There wasn't a chance I was staying off. Put a handful of Vaseline on it and let me back out there.

There was around 20 minutes left and Jonny Cooper got a bad knock and had to go off. Concussion. Denis Bastick came on for him, our last sub. Eoghan O'Gara could barely move. He was after doing some bad damage to his hamstring and all he could really do was sit on the edge of the square and tie one of their players up. Rory went down after a big collision. He got up and played on, but it turned out afterwards that he had a concussion too.

One minute we're on top and winning by a few points, the next you're looking around and thinking, 'Fuck's sake, we're all in bits here.'

As all of these injuries kept piling up, Mayo started to fight their way back into the game. Paul Flynn dropped in beside me, a multiple All-Star forward playing at full-back. Running repairs. Anything at all to get us over the line.

We got there. Mayo were two points down with a few seconds left when they got a free close to our goal. O'Connor put it over the bar, hoping to get one last chance for their equaliser, but as soon as Clucko kicked the ball out, that was it.

Through the hugs and the handshakes, I made my way up the steps of the Hogan Stand to collect my medal. John had promised that he would be home to celebrate with me the next time that I won an All-Ireland, but we never got the chance. I missed him that day more than ever. I lifted Sam Maguire and my big brother lifted it with me.

———

A few days after we beat Mayo, I flew out to Ibiza to meet Sarah. The two of us had known each other through friends for a long time before we ever started going out. There's a photo somewhere from after the 2011 final when myself and Flynner and James McCarthy brought Sam up to DCU to show it off. Sarah and her friend jumped in for a photo with the three of us and the cup.

We only started going out shortly before that 2013 All-Ireland. I had booked a trip out to Ibiza for the closing parties in October with a couple of the lads and, conveniently, she was going to be there with some of her friends at the same time. All I could think of was this big scar under my left eye, and the shiner that I had to go with it. Any doorman in his right mind was going to take one look at the state of me and tell me where to go.

It was grand though, I had a plan. I've always been into my fashion and that night after we beat Mayo, I decided to do something a little bit different for the celebration dinner. All of the lads showed up to the team hotel in their suits, and I came in wearing a dickie bow, braces, and a pair of big thick-rimmed non-prescription glasses. I don't care how much slagging I got off the rest of them, I looked well. And as a bonus, the glasses did a decent job of hiding the black eye, so they had to go in the bag and come over to Ibiza with me for the craic. I'd say Sarah was fit to turn and run that first night I walked into the club.

Thankfully, she didn't and we've been together ever since. She is an incredible person with such a huge heart, and without doubt one of the most thoughtful and generous people I know. She's the kind of person who if she saw a stray cat struggling at the side of the road, she would pick it up and bring it to the vet and then take it home again and stay up all night looking after it – and I can say that with confidence because it has happened.

She is intelligent, ambitious, and, above all, very supportive. If I wrote about half of the things that Sarah does for me and the sacrifices that she makes, she would deny it to the ground because that's the way she is, but I know I couldn't do it without her. The players are the ones in the spotlight and it's easy to focus on the long hours that we put in, but it's nothing really in comparison to the sacrifices that our partners make. Nights out, weekends, summer holidays – all of those things that should be a part of your normal life, they all go out the window. We're the ones that get all the glory at the end of it, but it's a team effort. I've been a part of three All-Ireland wins since I started going out with Sarah, and that is no coincidence at all.

There's an old philosophy exercise that helps you think about how you spend your time that I find very helpful. You imagine that you have a glass jar, empty, and beside it you have a pile of rocks, a pile of pebbles and a pile of sand. The rocks represent the things that are most important to you in life; they are the first thing to go into the jar and they take up most of the space. Then the pebbles represent your next most important priority; and then the sand, the little things, which take up the rest of the space.

If I look at that jar now, my sport and business commitments are the rocks taking up most of the space and my relationships are the pebbles. Carving out quality time for the important people in my life is something that I've always been bad at. I try to make an effort to stop in and see Dad on the way home from work a few times a week. He's retired now, and when I call in and sit down with him, all he wants to do is tell me about his day. And sometimes I just tune out. I'm so tired and mentally drained after work that when he wants to talk to me, I'm not there. What good is that?

When I was younger, I had that stereotypical 'male' relationship with Dad; I didn't hug him or tell him how much I loved him half as often as I should have. Now that he's getting older and I realise that I won't have him forever, I know how stupid that is. The more I get to know about his life, the more I come to appreciate what a positive person he is – no matter who he meets, there's always a joke – and what incredible experiences he's had.

'I want you to write down all of these stories,' I told him, 'so that they don't get forgotten and I can tell my own kids about their granda some day.'

I see how brilliant he is now with June and Lindy's kids, and I know that if I can be half the father to my children that he is to me, I'll have nothing to worry about.

The same goes for Mam. For years she was so used to having John call her a couple of times every week from London, and she'd put him on loudspeaker in the kitchen and just chat away to him about her day and his day while she cooked or cleaned. That's something big that has been missing from her life since John died, possibly more than any of us realise, and I know I should be making myself available a little bit more to call in to see her and chat to her. Sarah as well. She makes loads of sacrifices for me and I know I could be better at making time for her.

Not so long ago, being a footballer and playing for Dublin was my number one goal, and everything else was a distant second. Much as I still love football, I know that it's only one small part of a much bigger picture, and a part that can't last forever, no matter how hard I cling on to it. One of my big priorities now is to bring more balance to my life – to flip the glass jar so that my relationships are the rocks, and sport and business are the pebbles. Time is always going to be the tricky part. If I have a business meeting, I put it in my phone, but I never put in a meeting that I want to have with my family. There's the difference already.

It can be a bit of a catch-22. I always had an ambition of retiring Mam, I always wanted to work hard and grow my businesses to a level where I could give her back the financial support that her and Dad gave me, so that she could afford to give up her job if she wanted to. When you're working that hard to try to do that, it takes your time and energy away from the relationships, which is kind of stupid in a way – you're trying to have a better relationship with your parents, but you're trying to make more money to have a better relationship with your parents. If you asked Mam and Dad, they would be the first to say that it's not about the money, they would rather spend time with me.

It's the same with trying to make time for your other interests outside of sports and business, whether that's sitting down to watch a couple of episodes of *Game of Thrones* or – something that people might not know about me – finding time to practise the saxophone.

I took it up about two or three years ago. Mam was giving out because I'm very picky to buy presents for and I already have everything, apparently.

'Is there anything you'd actually like?' she asked me. 'I don't know what to be getting you.'

'Do you know what? I'd love to learn how to play a musical instrument,' I said. 'Will you buy me a saxophone and I'll learn it?'

She thought I was messing, but I was dead serious. We're a family that loves music and dancing, even though none of us play instruments. Growing up there was always music on in the flat, whether it was whatever pop or boybands the girls were listening to, or John and his rap, or a bit of dance music. We were all into dance, even Dad, and he still is. Any time he gets into my car now, all he wants to hear is whatever dance I'm listening to at the moment.

The sax is huge in house music and I knew it would be something different, as well as being a good hobby and a way to unwind from all of the other things going on my life. My sister bought me a few lessons to get me started and, for a couple of years, I was going once a week. Again, with football and the businesses, it was hard to find the time to practise as much as I needed. Plus, there aren't a huge amount of saxophone teachers in Dublin, so there was usually a good bit of commuting involved as well.

I've always promised myself that when I buy a house, I'll set aside an hour in the morning for 'Me Hour' – wake up early enough and get out of bed so that I've time to spend an hour doing something for myself before I've to go to work or training.

It could be food prep, meditation, or just setting out a plan for the day, and, hopefully, it will give me time for some early morning saxophone practice. I'll tell the new neighbours not to bother with an alarm clock.

We've had a great tradition at the last few All-Ireland home-comings that any of the players who fancy singing a song or playing a bit of music will do a bit for the fans. Kev McManamon started it off in 2011, I think. Kev and his brother Sean are crack-ing musicians, and he lives with Danny O'Reilly from The Coronas, so he never needs to be asked twice to get a sing-song started. He did a song by The Killers with Sean one year, and Van Morrison's 'Brown Eyed Girl' another year, and Dean Rock did 'I'm Gonna Be (500 Miles)' by The Proclaimers. I told Kev that hopefully one year we'll win the All-Ireland and we'll both be able to play, him on the guitar and me on the sax, jamming away with Sam Maguire sitting there beside us on the stage.

Sometimes you hear about the extremes that elite athletes go to fine-tune their skills, whether it's Michael Jordan taking 1,000 shots or Rory McIlroy hitting 1,000 balls every day. At the stage I'm at in my career now, finding and maintaining balance between all of the different components of my life is far more beneficial than any sort of repetitive practice. I know that if I can get that balance right, I'll be able to give 100% on the pitch. That's going to make me a more happy, positive person and, ultimately, a better player.

———

When I had nothing, winning meant everything to me. I built a world in which football was so central and so important, I didn't feel safe without it. I was scared that if I lost football, I would lose everything that was good in my life. Of course that wasn't true. Life brings us all much more significant losses and setbacks than anything that can happen on a football pitch.

Experience doesn't make losing any easier, but it does bring a new perspective; defeats hurt, but it doesn't mean that they're useless. When Donegal beat us in the All-Ireland semi-final in 2014, we learned a lot as players. Tactically, they had a game-plan that caught on us the hop. On the pitch, we didn't recognise the threat until it was too late, and we didn't adapt to it.

For the first 20 minutes, Donegal sat off and we pushed up on them. When they had possession, we didn't want them to have any space or time to work the ball out from defence. When we had it, we trusted that we would be able to get men free within shooting distance and kick points over the blanket rather than try to force our way through it. Flynner put one over from just inside the 45, Diarmuid Connolly kicked one from further back again. I sliced my first attempt high into the sky. When I got another chance a few minutes later, I didn't even think of carrying it any closer to goal. I took two steps and put my boot through it from about 40 metres. It put us five points up and we were in control.

It was only when we dropped off them and gave them a little bit of space that they started to get a bit more ambitious, come at us, and make a few chances. Before half time, they got a flukey enough goal, a scramble after a long ball into the square that we didn't really deal with.

Sitting in the dressing room at half time, we were a point down and asking ourselves why we had stopped pushing up on them when that had been working so well for us in the first 20 minutes. We went out and tried to do the same thing again, and that's when they caught us. We didn't recognise that their plan was to start hitting direct balls down the middle, with support runners in twos and threes lining up to join the attack at pace. We left too much space in behind us, and when they countered, they were able to outnumber us easily. Their three goals killed us and we were well beaten.

It was our first championship defeat under Jim and it hurt, but when you lose a game like that, there's no point in trying to hide. You have to own your mistakes. The responsibility that day fell entirely on the players who were out on the pitch, it was nothing to do with the management, and when we were asked questions about it afterwards, we had to face up to that fact. When Donegal changed the game, we didn't adapt as quickly as we should have. We knew that if we wanted to get back to an All-Ireland final the following year, that was something that we needed to improve on. That's the whole point of becoming tactically smarter – the more teams that throw different things at us, the more we learn, and the more opportunities we have to grow into a better and better team.

We have definitely grown, because even though we have lost games since that day, I haven't had the same feeling since, that a team has beaten us tactically on the pitch. We have to be confident in our preparation, our game-plan, and our abilities, and we have to understand that there are times in matches when the run of play will go against us. From the outside, it's easy to look at a game where a team gets on top against us for a period and think, that's the secret, that's how you break this Dublin team down. But the game is played at such a high level that every little mistake is magnified, and if we make two in quick succession, it's nearly seen as a full-blown crisis or systems failure. Teams see that and think that that's what they need to target to be successful against us. From our point of view, it's simple – there is no crisis. Instead, we have to be able to recognise when we've made a mistake, whether that's in the selection of the pass or the execution of the pass, and work to make sure it doesn't happen again.

There will be plenty more days when we come up against teams that put us to the pin of our collar tactically, like Donegal did in 2014. When it happens, we have to be ready to adapt. Lesson learned.

———

After the 2015 international rules game, Niall Morgan, the Tyrone goalkeeper, sent me a message.

'I thought you'd be a dick because of what you're like on the pitch, but you're actually sound.'

I burst out laughing when I read it. You're not the only one, Niall.

Anybody who knows me knows who I am and what I'm like. Ever since John died, my ambition in life is to go and help people every day. That might sound cheesy and clichéd and, to be honest, like PR bullshit to some people. It might be hard to match it up with the man you sometimes see on the pitch, but it's a fact and I'm grateful and delighted to do it. My profile as an athlete gives me a platform to help people; my businesses work to help people better themselves; and the charity I founded in 2016 will hopefully help thousands of people change their lives.

There's a selfishness to it too. I help people because it helps me. When I wake up in the morning, I feel that there's a purpose to my day beyond sport. I can go to bed at night happy that I'm making the most of the opportunities life has given me, opportunities that a lot of my friends and family didn't get.

Don't get me wrong. I'm far from perfect. I'm moody and I'm

stubborn and there are plenty of times when I come across as a bit of a know-it-all. I'm not Ned Flanders – and even he's not perfect – but when I wake up in the morning, I try to be positive and I try to help others, which is as much as anyone can do.

Once I cross that white line, I'm a different animal. I would never claim otherwise. I can be aggressive on the pitch at times. That's my style. It's something that I'm good at. It's something that I've built on over the years, probably starting from the days when I was playing minor – maybe even younger than that, when I was wrecking Paddy Christie's head by getting into stupid scraps during games. It's something that works for me. That's how I play and it has helped me to be more successful than I ever thought possible. Why would I go and change it?

In a way, there's a respect to it. I'm going to try and rile you up, and if that puts you off your game that easily, fair enough. But if you respond like I expect you to respond, and I bring out the best in you, I'm going to have to be at my best to mark you and keep you quiet. I'm not the guy who is asking the ref to dish out the black cards and red cards. I'm the guy who wants to mark the best player on the pitch, at their best, so that I can see how good I am as a footballer.

That's what I am. A footballer.

A few days ahead of the 2015 All-Ireland final, I got my assignment: Colm Cooper. In the run-up to any game, once management tell you that you're starting and who they want you to line up against, your mind switches on. You really start to do your homework. You're dropping off a delivery to a customer or driving from one meeting to another and different thoughts pop into your head. Everybody prepares differently, but one thing I like to do is mentally draw up a list of questions – not that I want to ask myself, but that I want to ask of the man that I'm going up against.

Cooper is one of the most high-profile players of the last 10 or 15 years, one of the best footballers of his generation. No matter who he is, my number one job that day boiled down to the same thing it always does: keep him quiet. That's hardly revolutionary tactical thinking – as if no defender has ever marked Colm Cooper and thought, 'I'll try to keep this lad quiet today.' But all of these players who have tried and failed before – what have they done when they're marking him? What questions have they asked? Because with all due respect, whatever they were doing, a lot of it didn't work.

I knew that the way to play him was to take him outside his comfort zone, and to do that, I had one question that I wanted to ask him: can you defend? He's a player who has changed games in an instant, and if I went out and played like a traditional corner-back, I'd be giving him free rein to spend most of the game in the parts of the pitch he wants to be in. Of course he's comfortable when he's on the front foot and attacking. What's he like when he's going the other way?

Whenever I got a chance that day, I pushed out of defence. Towards the end of the first half, we won a turnover at the back. As we got the ball, I was a good 30 yards ahead of the play and so was he. Instead of funnelling back as cover and allowing him to follow me, I forced him to come back towards his own goal with me. Ciarán Kilkenny saw me make a run out towards the wing and handpassed it. I took one solo, shaped as if I was going back inside, came back out onto my right, and kicked a point. It was the only score either of us had that day. Job done.

That year, 2015, was when I felt that I really evolved as a Dublin player and brought a new attacking dimension to my game. I have been very fortunate to play inter-county football under Jim Gavin and a management team that allows all of us to express ourselves as footballers, and actively encourages it. I know that I have these capabilities in me, but different managers have different styles, and there's no guarantee that you'll be allowed to show them. If I was playing under a manager that wouldn't allow me go forward or wouldn't allow me do certain things, I'd be the same old corner-back, sitting there, passing the ball off to the next man as soon as I got it.

The cameras picked up on myself and Cooper having a few words at the end of the game and for days and weeks after, in nearly every interview, people wanted to know what was said. There was nothing to it really. From my perspective, he plays a certain way to win games for his team, and so do I, and I explained that to him. We shook hands and that was the end of it.

There have been a couple of incidents over the years that people took exception to, or that blew up after the game. It comes with the territory. You'd do well to play nine seasons as an inter-county defender and not be involved in a couple of rows. The exact same things happen in games all around the country every single week, but if it happens in a big game, with thousands in the stadium and maybe hundreds of thousands more watching on TV, it gets highlighted. If it happens more than once, that's when you start to get a reputation. Some incidents look different when you slow them down or speed them up or zoom in or zoom out. The game isn't played through a camera lens though, is it?

Sometimes people jump to conclusions. Sometimes they get it wrong. And then sometimes you do things and immediately you think – that was a mistake, I didn't actually mean to do that, it was just the heat of the moment. Of course tempers run high at the time, but I've clashed with lads and met them down the line, shared lifts with them at All-Star ceremonies, and it's all been water under the bridge. I've done the wrong thing and been sent off a couple of times. I've been given a couple of one-match bans. They're the rules of the game, and if you play the game on the edge, you accept that. I'm never going to win a popularity contest and that doesn't bother me.

Winning isn't everything but I still play sport to win, and I do things on the pitch to win. If we win matches, we win medals, and the more medals I have, the more of a profile I have and the more people I can help. If I do something and there are implications that hurt my team and my teammates in any way, then I know it was the wrong decision. That's all that matters really. I'm at a stage in my career where I've won a lot and I'm very grateful for what I've won. Now it's about enjoying it and seeing how far I can go, challenging myself to play outside of myself and pushing myself to be better and better.

———

We were that close to the stage, you could nearly reach out and touch the strings on Damien Dempsey's guitar. The Axis in Ballymun must be one of the most intimate venues in the country for a gig.

I hadn't really listened to a lot of Damo's music. The closest I'd come was at the All-Ireland homecoming in 2011 when Kev Mc rewrote the lyrics to 'Sing All Our Cares Away' to include the names of all of the team and sang it on stage the night after we beat Kerry. The Dublin lads love Damo. They were the ones who put me on to him, and I could see why. He's a phenomenal storyteller, a poet, and if you've grown up in Dublin, it's hard not to listen to his songs and fit your life into them. It takes real skill for an artist to connect with a person and take them to a place deep inside themselves. Damo has it in abundance. Now when I'm getting ready on match day, there are always a few of his songs on the playlist.

I've been hooked on his music since the night when I first saw him live, in the Axis. My sister Kellie came with me. There was a girl sitting a row or two in front of us, and in between songs, she was roaring up at him on the stage.

'"Ghosts of Overdoses".' She shouted again. 'Play "Ghosts of Overdoses". You have to play it. You're in Ballymun.'

I'd never heard the song and my first instinct was – that's a bit cheeky. I don't know if she was from Ballymun, or if she had any connection, but I was a bit taken aback. And then Damo played the opening chords and started to sing and I understood.

*Hey little baby, I want to take you from here*
*Hey little baby, I don't want to see you on the gear,*
*It's so hard to find your way back.*
*Hey little baby, it's every parent's worst fear*
*For their child to end up on smack.*

This place that he was singing about, this was my home. I sat there with shivers, my sister beside me, and listened to this painting of a world we knew so well, the pills and needles. With every carefully chosen word, another memory of the place that we had grown up in and loved, the good and the bad. Our childhood, our family, our pain, our brother.

*Now I walk along these streets,*
*All the ghosts, they walk their beats,*
*Up to flats and into stairwells*
*Where they lie in heroin hell.*
*Little kids, they walk right through them.*
*I just hope they don't become them.*

It wasn't just John. I knew so many of those ghosts. They lived on my street and around the corner and went to my school. I knew them from the shops and the swimming pool and the youth club. I threw stones with them and I threw stones at them. Ghosts of people that I played football with and played football against, ghosts of people who stood there and watched because they had nowhere else to be as night crept in. Ghosts everywhere.

Life took me far beyond Ballymun, all over Ireland and all over the world, but I never left. When I moved out of home, I got my own place five minutes up the road. A couple of days after we beat Kerry in the 2015 All-Ireland final, I stood in front of the last of the towers and looked up. The last physical link to the old Ballymun. Once they pulled it down a few weeks later, all we would have left were the memories.

The work had already started and the cranes had already moved in but we wanted to get one last photograph. Not for the wall. For the newspaper. The photographer from *The Irish Times* looked at me, and then looked at the steel fence that was blocking our way, and then looked back at me.

'What do you reckon?' she said. 'We can do it here alright but it's not going to look great with this fence in the way.'

'Gimme a sec,' I told her.

The season was over and I had no interest in talking about football. This article wasn't going to be about the All-Ireland though. It was going to be about Ballymun, another attempt to change the conversation, to show the young people of the area that you could be from this place and go on to achieve great things, and that the help and support was there for them.

I spotted a man on the other side of the fence and wandered over towards him. If he could get in, then surely so could we. As I got closer, I realised I knew him. He lived around the corner from us when I was younger. His son, Billy, was the brilliant footballer who first taught me how to play as a kid on the street.

He was working as security on the site, and I explained to him what we were there to do, and what the article was going to be about.

'Is there any chance that we could just go in a couple of yards there and take two or three photos to go with this article?'

He opened up a gap for us. 'Of course, go on in.'

I hadn't seen him for a while and we chatted for a minute as he let us through. Billy had died not long before that, of an overdose, another life lost to drugs in Ballymun.

If drugs hadn't killed the people that we grew up with, crime got a lot of them in the end. Mountjoy Prison is quite an intimidating place, even if you've done nothing wrong. The paranoia that you get sometimes going through airport security, wondering if you've done something thick – it's like that, only double. There are times when I've walked in and the most stupid stuff starts running through my head. I see the sniffer dogs, and then I immediately think about the last time that I was in contact with a drug addict, and then I'm thinking, can they smell that off me, do they think I have drugs?

I show my ID to the security officer and hand over the bag I've brought with me so that he can check to make sure that there's nothing in it other than a new Dublin training top and knicks still in their plastic. He pushes the little tray towards me, and I empty my pockets and go through the metal detector. When that's all done, then I'm allowed to go down the corridor and into the small private visiting room.

I go up to see Steo whenever I can. He's been one of my best mates since we were kids, and we always had that strong connection when we were growing up. We were the two lads that weren't drinking when everybody else was, and we kept each other away from the serious trouble that our friends were getting sucked into. We drifted apart as we got a little bit older, and unfortunately he got caught up in the wrong sort of business with the wrong sort of people. He made a bad mistake a few years ago, got caught, and ended up in jail for his part in a robbery.

Prison is no place to have to go to visit your best friend, but that's a sad fact of life for a lot of people I know. When I do get the chance to go up to see Steo, we just sit and chat. There's not much else you can really do when you're in prison. I know that he just wants to see his mate and talk to him, and I'm the exact same, but in the back of my mind I can't shake that little bit of anxiety when he asks about what's going on my life. Or he'll ring me, and I never want to say that I'm doing too well because I'm so conscious of how tough it must be in there for him.

'Any craic with you anyway?'

'Not much, no. I'm heading off to Spain in two weeks' time with Sarah but other than that …'

That's the exact opposite of what he needs to hear. His are long and lonely days, especially when he has a family and a young son waiting for him to get out. He's trying to do the right thing for them now. He accepted his mistake, pleaded guilty to the crime in court, and is doing everything he can to make sure he gets early release.

Our paths may have gone two different ways for the moment, but when he does get out, I've told him that I will be here to help him in whatever way I can with whatever he needs. Everybody makes mistakes, and his don't mean that I care any less about him. Who am I to judge him for that? I make mistakes all the time myself.

There are so many people who have made mistakes over the years, especially in Ballymun, and when they get out of prison, they end up making the same ones over and over again because that's the life that they are used to and they don't have the tools to turn it around. I know Steo is smarter than that. Any qualifications that he's able to do while he's locked up, he's doing them, and judging by the condition he's in, he's spending the rest of his time in the prison gym. He has so much potential that he hasn't been able to use because of the choices he made. I know he can put this behind him, and I'll be there to help him do it. I know if things were the other way around, he'd be the first one there to do the same for me.

Steo, Davey, Mossy, Doc, Joycey, Cathal, my teammates – outside my family, they are the people who are closest to me. They are the people that I know I can rely on if I ever need help, if I ever need anything, and it works both ways. Loyalty is everything to me.

———

The passage of time couldn't heal Ballymun's drug problem. The tide rose and fell, but drugs never went away completely. More than 20 years after John took his first hit of heroin, young people in the area are still being tempted down the same dark pathways, still making the same mistakes that he did.

When I started to rebuild my life after John's death, I challenged myself to find a new purpose, to go out and make a real difference beyond what I was doing on the football pitch and in business. Losing him awoke this drive in me, to stop thinking about myself so much and start thinking about what I could do to help others. The community in Ballymun had always been so supportive of me over the years, in every aspect of my life, and now I was in a position where I could be doing more to give back to the area. I wanted to make sure that not a single family in Ballymun would ever again have to go through what my family had gone through. The same traps and pitfalls still existed, but after living through John's struggle with him, I knew that I could go some small way towards helping to break that cycle.

I'm always happy to go down and give a talk in the Comp. After all the messing I did there over the years, it's the least I can do. Ger McLoughlin got in touch with me back in 2012. He was working with a community organisation called the Ballymun–Whitehall Area Partnership, and they had set up an enterprise group in the school for any of the kids that were interested. Ger really believed in the young people of Ballymun. He could see that they were intelligent and innovative, and they just needed a little bit more support to channel their skills and let them flourish. I went down and I told them about some of my experiences.

Myself and Ger got chatting after the talk. I started thinking out loud.

'There's so much more we could be doing here, Ger, a fitness course maybe. Not for the kids that I'm talking to today, but for kids when they leave school, 18 to 24, that age. It would be great if we had something in the community for them. I'd love to do something like that.'

I was already getting excited by the prospect.

Ger was nodding away with a bit of a smile. 'It's funny actually that you say that. We've been talking about targeting something like that this year. Leave it with me for a while and I'll come back to you.'

True to his word, he was back to me a few months later. 'Philly, the fitness course we were talking about. Are you interested?'

I was, absolutely. Together, myself and Ger sat down and started to draw up the criteria for the course. We wanted to target young people in the Ballymun–Whitehall area, aged 18–24, who had been on social welfare for longer than a year. Because the programme was being run through the Department of Social Protection, we were able to get a list of everybody that met that criteria. There was somewhere between 500 and 700 people that matched up, I think, and we sent every one of them a mailshot to see if they were interested.

We called the course Philly McMahon's Kaizen Evolution. 'Kaizen' is Japanese for continual improvement, and I loved that – isn't that the philosophy we should be trying to live our lives by every day? The hope was that if we put my name to it, as an example of someone from the area who had made the choice to stay in education and develop new skills, that would help to draw people to the course. It did. We got 50 responses, which was as good as we could have hoped, narrowed it down to 30 interviews, and filled 20 places on the course.

When I walked into the room with the 20 of them the first day, there wasn't a sound. The whole lot of them wouldn't say a word to each other. Once the course was up and running, my main role was to deliver the strength and conditioning seminar, but I got to know all of these people and their stories. Some of them had been in trouble with the law, some of them with drugs, some of them were struggling with their sexuality, some were going through bereavement – but no matter what difficulties they had in their life, they were there because they wanted to improve themselves. By the end of the 20 weeks, when I walked into the room, I could hardly get them to shut up. They were singing, dancing, messing, and so much more confident in themselves to a point where they were getting up and teaching in front of each other.

Unfortunately, there's always a small percentage of any group that you're never going to help – some people just have it in their heads that the world owes them something – but when you look at the numbers from that course, it was a massive success. Seven of the 20 went on to further education and six went on to employment. That's a huge success rate by any standard.

Look at it from the government's perspective. If someone aged 18–24 is entitled to €144 in social welfare payments a week, and we help 13 of them into employment or education, that's not far off €100,000 a year in savings. And the studies show that people who are on social welfare for a year are likely to be on it for two or three years, so that amount of money starts getting bigger very quickly.

I was delighted with the progress we had made. We had created something from scratch that had a real, practical impact on people's lives. It was a no-brainer for me to run the course again for a second year, but when we went back to apply for the same funding, we couldn't get it. The system had changed, private companies were being encouraged to tender for the courses, and the Ballymun–Whitehall Area Partnership lost the bid. Ger had been the workhorse that made the course such a success, but with no budget to work with, he moved on to other projects. We were back to square one.

———

I pulled up outside my house and reached over to the passenger seat to grab Sam Maguire – that's something that you'll never get tired of doing. I had been asked to give a talk in one of the local youth clubs that morning and I wanted to bring it with me.

That trophy is like the bat signal for kids. I didn't even have the car door closed and I was already surrounded. Photos and autographs and selfies.

I went inside to have a bit of breakfast and when I came back out to head down to the talk, another young lad came running over to me, the younger brother of one of the kids who had been with me a few minutes earlier.

'Aw, I didn't get your autograph,' he said, so I called him over.

He said to me, 'Are you famous?'

I didn't really know what to say.

'Ehhhhhh, I don't know,' I said to him. In my head, I was saying, 'No, of course not,' but I was looking at him, and I knew that if I said no to him, he'd be distraught.

Before I even had a chance to answer him, he said, 'Are you on telly?'

That was a much easier question. 'Ah yeah,' I said. 'I'm on telly. I suppose I am famous a little bit.'

Without missing a beat, he said, 'How can you be famous if you're from Ballymun?'

That was the moment when it hit me. Not that being from Ballymun in 2015 was still seen as something that limited your opportunities or potential, or that a kid of that age was already thinking that way, but that I was now in a position where I could have some sort of positive influence on that lie. Dublin football had put me in a position where I could say, 'Yes I'm from Ballymun, yes I'm famous, and if you're from Ballymun too, you can do whatever it is you want in life.' The kid never used the words 'role model', but it was the first time that I ever felt like one. And once you accept that you have that status in certain people's eyes, you have to make a decision about what you're going to do with it.

So the two of us sat down. It would have made a great picture, the two of us on the side of the road and the Sam Maguire there beside us. I just talked to him, and told him a little bit about who I was, where I had grown up, and what it was that I did now that made me famous. He didn't need a lecture on the good and bad of the world. He just needed one little thought that would help him, a kid from Ballymun, see his world a little bit differently, and that was what I tried to give him.

When we were finished, I headed down to the youth club, late for the talk, and as I walked in, some young lad ran into the room and shouted, 'Fuck the guards.'

I pulled him aside.

'Why did you say that?' I asked him.

'I dunno, I dunno, I'm sorry,' he said.

I wasn't letting him away with it that easily.

'What happens if your house gets robbed or if someone tries to rob you or they hit your mam or your dad – who are you going to call to help you?'

He knew where I was going with this, but he was stubborn enough.

'Awww, I'll do it meself,' he said.

So I said to him, 'What happens if the person is bigger and bolder and stronger than you – what would you do then?'

He was trying not to say it, but he couldn't avoid it.

'I'd call the guards,' he said.

I said to him, 'Yeah – so why are you thinking that they're your enemy?'

I met those two kids within the space of 20 minutes. I had planned to tell a completely different story at the youth club, but when I walked into the room to give the talk, I just told them the story about the little fella up outside my house, and thinking that you can't be famous or popular or whatever if you come from Ballymun. It worked really well. And then I mentioned the conversation I'd just had with the lad shouting abuse at the guards, and again, it seemed to have a really big impact on these kids. As it turned out, that kid had been on probation. A couple of weeks later, I bumped into one of the local guards and he told me that something so simple as me talking to that kid for a minute or two had made a massive difference in his attitude and in his behaviour.

I don't think anyone ever sets out to become a role model, and everybody's role model is different, but I certainly know that when you have that sort of profile and position where people are looking up to you, there's an obligation to be positive and supportive in whatever way you can. For me, that means being myself and using my own life experiences as a way of helping people within my community.

I mentioned this to Siobhan Earley, who is the player development manager with the Gaelic Players Association. Siobhan was the person who first suggested that I look into working with a personal development coach. Even the words 'personal development coach', or the suggestion that something like that can be coached, will put some people off, but I felt that if it was going to help me, even a little bit, it was worth doing.

There's an American psychologist, Carol Dweck, and she has a theory of 'growth mindset' – that the most successful people are the ones who know that their personality and their abilities aren't set in stone, but something that you can work on to change and improve as you go through life. That's how I like to see myself.

I realised that I was in situations – in sport, in my businesses, and now in life more generally – where I had the power to help people. It's something that I love doing, talking to people and trying to give them one good thing to take away from the conversation. I love that feeling and I wanted to know what more I could be doing. Right there, that was an opportunity to grow and Siobhan was right, a personal development coach could help me to do that.

When you sit down with a personal development coach, they try to get you to look at your life a bit more deeply and reflect on what you do and why you do it. They're there to help you to figure out who you are as a person and who you want to be, and then they try to give you some focus and direction.

Again, I told my coach the story about the kid on the path outside my house. When I was done, he said, 'Now you've seen the impact that you have as a role model. How did helping that kid make you feel?'

I was honest with him. 'I must have grown about two or three inches taller when I did it,' I said.

'That feeling you got,' he said, 'that buzz you got. Imagine scaling that and magnifying that so it's not just that little bit of path outside your house, but it's a big massive path, and you're trying to get as many people onto that path as you can so that you can help them. That's your meaning. That's what you should be going after.

'If helping one person gave you such a good feeling,' he said, 'imagine what will happen if you get loads and loads of people onto this path.'

That's what I've been trying to do ever since.

———

In February 2016, I went on *The Late Late Show* and, with Mam and Dad sitting there in the audience, I spoke at length and in detail about John, his struggle with drugs, his death, and the impact that it had on our family. I never shied away from talking about John whenever the subject came up in interviews, but for a lot of people watching that night, it was the first time that they had heard me speak about this side of my life, the side they never saw. Once I started to share my story, and John's story, and tell people about my Half Time Talk idea, more and more people started to open up and share their own stories with me.

Sinead is a member in one of my gyms. I first met her back in 2013 when she signed up to the Kaizen Evolution course as one of the original 20, but it was only much later that I got to know her and what was going on in her life. She is a perfect example of the Half Time Talk in action. She has had a very difficult life but her attitude to her problems has been an inspiration, to say the least.

Sinead lost two members of her family at a young age and in a very short space of time. Her brother was messing on the back of a truck, as lots of young lads do, and he fell off and hit his head and tragically passed away. Not long after that, her mother jumped off the flats and took her own life. Her older brother moved away, and her father and younger brother both struggled with their bereavements. Sinead became the backbone of her family, shouldering a massive amount of responsibility.

She used that fitness course as her Half Time Talk. Rather than let her problems drag her down, which would have been very easy to do, she saw an opportunity and seized it to push on in life. On the back of her determination and all of her hard work, she is employed now, and she is going back to do more fitness training. Seeing her turn her life around gave me huge added motivation to help people.

Sinead then came to me and asked me to speak to her brother, to see if there was anything I could do to help him. I spoke to him and told him my story, told him about the power that each of us has to wake up in the morning and decide that things will be different, no matter what has gone before and no matter what problems we're dealing with. And then I listened to him.

Then there was a lad who phoned me one night, not long after I started to speak publicly about John. An Irish guy living in Hamburg.

'It was great to hear about your life,' he said. 'I'm struggling myself at the minute.'

He told me about his brother who had died that Christmas from an overdose, and the depression he had felt himself since.

We must have been on the phone for the best part of an hour, and he was the one doing all of the talking while I just sat and listened. He told me all of this and I said to him, 'Look, I'm going to help you in whatever way I can, but I'm only going to do that for you if you promise me that you will tell somebody else the story that you told me just now. It could be tomorrow, it could be in a couple of weeks, but you have got to tell somebody.'

He did more than that. He went away and set up a charity fundraiser, a seven-a-side GAA tournament in Hamburg.

There was another woman who called.

'I saw your interview,' she said. 'Can I get my son to come to one of your talks?'

I explained to her that, at that stage, I had only really spoken to a handful of journalists about it and that I didn't do public talks.

'Can I pay you to talk to him?' she said.

I didn't want money, but she was obviously determined to get me to speak to him. I wasn't interested if it was something that she wanted. I needed to know that it was something that he wanted.

'Get him to give me a ring,' I said, and he did and he told me his story.

This guy had developed a cocaine addiction, which started off in social settings, once a week, and gradually got worse until he was using most days, and it had driven a wedge between him and his family. He wanted to work to repair the damage he had done and get his life back on track. He wanted to get back talking to his wife. He wanted to starting playing Gaelic football with his club again.

When we finished our conversation, again, I told him my side of the deal: I would help, but now he had to go and tell someone else his story. I wanted him to understand the power of the choices he was making, not just for himself, but also in the way that they could help to change somebody else's life for the better. He went back to playing with the club and he rang me a few weeks later to tell me that he had spoken about his experiences to his teammates. One of the younger players in the squad came up to him later that evening and thanked him for sharing the story.

'I'm struggling with depression,' the young player said, 'and it's huge to hear someone talk about the problems that they've come through.'

The senior lad asked him to do the same thing, that when he was ready, he would promise to tell his own story to another person.

We all have the power to make a change in our lives, but just as much, we all have the power to help others. It starts with talking and with listening.

———

He brings John into it and, for a second, the mention of his name is like being punched.

'Your brother was only a junkie anyway.'

Ask anyone that I've ever marked: I do plenty of talking on the pitch myself. All players have little tricks, things that they do that will get inside their opponent's head, and you're just watching then for the reaction. It's like Conor McGregor looking into an opponent's eyes after he lands that first punch, waiting for that first hint of fear. Every player does it in their own way, whatever you think will work to get inside your man's head and get him to think differently. If you can introduce that little bit of anger or doubt or fear that takes up a tiny fraction of his thought process for the next few minutes, that's a tiny fraction less that he's thinking about the game. That's all it is, and at the end of it, you shake hands and walk away.

It's all part of the psychology of the game. If someone slags my girlfriend, my ma, my da, whatever it is, that's the kind of stuff that I've dealt with on the streets for my entire life. That's nothing new. I'll do whatever I can, too, to help my team win. Sometimes I do things and I go to places that other people won't. Because I can. Because I've no fear of going to those places. Because I know it works. But I know where I draw the line, and I know the things that I will not say and will not do. Racism, illness, bereavement – they're places I will never go to.

Sometimes it happens unintentionally, somebody makes a comment and they don't really know about what's going on in your life. But there are lads there who will do it from a place of pure malice because they think that's what's going to work. They know your brother has passed away, and they know he had an addiction, and they say your brother's a junkie and he died from an overdose, which he didn't. That's when I know – I have you now. You are that desperate to get to me that you have had to sink that low, to those depths.

He mentions John and my reaction is the exact opposite to what he intended. I hear this and it gives me 50% more energy.

Every time I feel tired, it's ringing in my ears. By the time it's all over, I've had one of my best-ever games.

———

When you lose someone to addiction, it's impossible not to think about the things that you should or shouldn't have done, or that you would do differently if you had a chance to start over. The important thing that I learned was to try to let go of any guilt and recriminations because they were useless, they weren't going to change anything, but I started to think more deeply about addiction, why it happens and how we deal with it, as individuals, as families, and as a society.

I read whatever I could get my hands on, books and articles and studies and government reports, but no matter how much information you have, it can still be hard to make sense of the actual experience that you have lived through. The only thing that I knew for sure was that John couldn't break his addiction and part of that was down to him and part of that was down to society. He tried to get clean for years, but never managed to do it for long.

I want to believe that when he wrote that last letter before he died, he meant what he said about going into rehab once and for all, that he was ready to turn his life around. Of course as his family we want to believe that, but we don't know. There are drug addicts in the world who will be drug addicts forever, until they die. But even if that is the case, that doesn't mean that we should turn our backs on them and abandon them. Surely our priority should be to keep them on this planet for as long as possible. The more days a drug addict has, the more days he or she has to turn their life around and become a recovered addict.

Siobhan Earley sent me a link to a YouTube video. It was a TED Talk by Johann Hari entitled 'Everything you think you know about addiction is wrong'. Siobhan knew a title like that would grab my attention. I sat down and pressed play. As I watched this video, so many of the points Hari was making resonated with me and matched up with what I had seen in John's life and death. He explained how patients in hospital are prescribed courses of diamorphine – pure heroin – often over long spells, but they don't become addicted in the same way that we expect street users to in a comparatively short space of time. He explained how we think of addiction as a chemical dependency, but it might actually be better to think of addiction as a reaction to our environment; that addicts turn to drugs like heroin as an escape from the world because they feel isolated and disconnected and marginalised from everyday life as it goes on around them. If that's true, it has massive implications for drug policy, because in the vast majority of Western countries in the world, our policies of stigmatisation and criminalisation push drug users further into their addiction.

'The opposite of addiction is not sobriety,' Hari finished. 'The opposite of addiction is connection.'

I had lived with that stigma, when that lad slagged me in the pool hall that night or when my opponent called my dead brother a junkie to try to get inside my head. I had internalised it and started to spread it myself, when I ignored my own brother because of his problems and walked past him on the street.

In 2015 and 2016, as I won my third and fourth All-Irelands with Dublin, my profile started to increase. People that I had never met knew my face and my name, they wanted to stop me and say hello on the street. More than that, I realised that a lot of these people cared about what I had to say, especially once I started to speak more and more about addiction. It wasn't just kids who looked up to me because I was good at football, or people from Ballymun who thanked me because I was a good ambassador for their community. It was broader than that.

I realised that John deserved more, that this country could have done more for him, and can be doing more for the addicts that are still alive out there and trying to get clean. I realised that I had a platform, and I could help to start that change. I decided to be an activist for drug addicts and to work to improve the policies that we have in this country for dealing with drugs and drug addiction. I wanted to question what's going on so that people are constantly trying to improve our relationship with drug addicts and families of drug addicts in this country. I've seen people in Ballymun and I've seen the joy on their faces when their loved ones come off drugs. It's an amazing feeling, and for me, it feels like that addict is part of my own family. When I see someone that has become clean, it's spine-tingling, it's inspirational, because I never got the chance to experience that with John.

One of the members in my gym, a recovered addict himself, pulled me aside one day.

'Philly, do you mind if I bring up a mate with me the next day to see how he gets on? I think it would be really good for him.'

'Yeah,' I said. 'Who is it?'

When he told me his friend's name, I thought he must have got it wrong. I knew this guy, had seen him only a couple of weeks earlier, and he was struggling so badly with drugs, I thought he was on the way out. He really looked like he was at death's door. I told him to bring him up, of course, and we'd have a look to see what we could do.

Electric is the only way to describe the feeling I got when the lad walked through the door a few days later. It was the closest

I've ever felt to that emotion you get at the final whistle of a winning All-Ireland.

'Woah. What the fuck?'

He was like a totally different person, clean and starting to turn his life around. I was absolutely stunned. I went over to say hello and shake his hand, and I told him that I'd seen him on the street not that long ago.

'What did you do?' I asked him. 'How did you do it?'

What he said to me was the best analogy I've ever heard.

He said, 'Philly, it's like waking up every morning and fighting Mike Tyson, and one morning, you wake up, and you say I don't want to fight you any more. You just have to take that decision.'

For a lot of addicts, getting themselves to a place where they can take that decision is a whole other battle in itself. The harsh reality is that not everybody will make it that far, but our entire attitude towards drugs and addiction needs to be a help, not a hindrance.

Smoking is an addiction. Alcoholism is an addiction. Gambling is an addiction. Eating disorders are an addiction. Why do we treat practically every addiction as a health issue, but drug addiction as a crime? That's where the stigma starts – because it's a crime, it's dirty, and it's something to hide and be embarrassed about. The reality is that there is a close link between drug use and mental health. Some people choose to take drugs purely for pleasure, and some people choose to take them so that they can escape some other pain in their life.

In my head, whenever I thought about John's choice to take drugs, I always thought about the external factors – growing up in Ballymun at the height of the heroin epidemic; falling in with a group of friends who were all experimenting and chasing highs; the lack of a positive role model in his life. Did John have some other pain that he was hiding from? I'm not sure. Maybe he did.

My dad is not John's dad. For as long as I've been alive, John's biological dad wasn't really a part of his life, very rarely around aside from showing up at Christmas time with a present or two under his arm. He and Mam split up years and years ago, after Kellie was born, and that's when Mam met Dad; I was born a few years later. I'm sure there are people from split homes who turn to drugs and other substances to deal with their pain, but I never thought that was the case for John. My dad was always there for him from a very young age; he was his dad, essentially.

When I decided that I wanted to tell John's story in full, I realised that there was a lot about his life that I still didn't know, even now. That was largely down to the difference in age between the two of us and my parents trying to protect me, but I also discovered that, as a family, there were some details that we just didn't know with any great certainty. Quite often, we'll draw a blank when it comes to connecting an event to a specific date or time. One year bleeds into the next and into the next, inseparable in the haze of emotional trauma. When was it that he first moved over to London? Had he been at home for my 21st birthday or was that Kellie's? Was it five years that he was in jail, or more, or less? Even at his most open, John kept things hidden from us as well and, in my case at least, there is a lot that I didn't know simply because I pushed him away and never knew how to talk to him properly, even as we both got older.

I sat down with Mam one afternoon, and we started to talk, reminiscing about happy stories and funny stories and sad ones. It's something that we don't do nearly enough as a family, but it was very therapeutic for both of us. Mam immediately started planning a party in John's memory, a celebration of his life, where everybody could come together and talk about him as if he was still here with us.

'What age did you know he was at it from?' I asked her.

'The drugs, I think 17,' she said. 'Definitely 17 for drugs. Before that, it was the hash, but 17 for the heavier drugs he was on.'

A few weeks later I called over to see Mick, John's old friend, and we sat down and caught up for well over an hour. He's doing well for himself now, has always stayed in touch with our family, and he could tell some stories about John. The two of them drifted apart as they got older. When Mick forced himself to get clean, John couldn't, and they couldn't be around each other.

A lot of the stories Mick told me that day reinforced the positive memories I have of John, my kind-hearted, protective, proud older brother. We started talking about how they had both ended up taking drugs at such a young age. It was Mick who told me about the first time that they used heroin, 14 years old in a battered Ballymun lift, the naivety to think that it was liquid hash.

'Oh, God.'

Mam took a deep breath, almost involuntarily, when she heard this story from me for the first time, the fresh detail too raw and too vivid. It had all started so much earlier than she could have ever imagined, from a place of confusion and childish innocence that she could never have expected.

It was Mick who told me about the rips and the crime and the fights that followed in their later teenage years. It was Mick who told me about bumping into John when he was on his way home from the clinic in Bray, a full week's supply of methadone in his inside jacket pocket.

I put it to him. 'A lot of drug addicts, they find that it's an escape,' I said. 'It gets you away from certain pain that you have.'

Mick remembered all the days when the two of them would go into town together, and John would want to call up to see his dad, but when they did, he never had much time for John. With the two oldest girls, June and Lindy, he usually made a bit more of an effort, but when John appeared, he'd give him a few pound and then send him on his way just as quickly. If there was a fight for attention and affection, he had already lost it.

'John had that little thing in him, Philly, where I think sometimes he felt isolated,' Mick said.

I'm still not sure. It's another one of those questions that we'll never know the answer to, because we'll never be able to ask John. If none of his friends were using drugs, and he was the only one, you might look to that as an explanation. Or if he was seven years younger and missed the worst of the heroin epidemic when he was growing up, like I did, and still fell into addiction, then you might see it as a reason. But because so many of John's friends ended up on the same destructive path, and from such a young age, it's hard to feel that it was caused by anything but their environment.

Years into his addiction, John's nanny died – his biological dad's mam. John really wanted to be there at the funeral that day, felt it was important. On the way out to the graveyard, John walked to the funeral car to get in with the rest of the family.

'There's no room in the limo, John,' he was told, and he had to sit in one of the cars behind.

That has stuck in my head to this day. Tormented by his addiction, John still wanted to do something nice to try to support that side of the family, even if he didn't have much of a relationship with them. The same loving, caring John had never gone away.

———

In 2016 I was invited to speak at an event in Dublin to launch a public consultation on the new National Drugs Strategy for Ireland. Normally I don't like speaking with notes, I don't feel that I need them, but I wrote this speech in advance and brought it with me. I knew the story I wanted to tell. I had told it plenty of times, and in front of much larger audiences than this, but this process had the potential to change Ireland's approach to drugs and addiction, and I wanted to make sure I got my message across without any confusion.

I unfolded my notes, cleared my throat, and started to speak.

'We are losing the war on drugs in Ireland.'

It was probably the toughest speech I've ever made. I was nervous as I started to talk, and explained John's addiction and the impact that it had on me growing up.

'I grew up constantly trying to hide my dirty secret, that of having a brother who was a drug addict,' I said. 'I believed that tough love was the way to deal with this stigma. I was embarrassed by him and so ignored him on the streets and never invited him to special events in case he showed me up. When I should have shown him empathy, compassion, and love, I turned the other way.'

It was the first time that I ever publicly admitted that I was embarrassed by John, ashamed to be his brother, because he was an addict. I didn't realise how emotional the speech was until I looked up from the notes and looked out into the audience. All of these faces were staring back at me, and I could see people nearly starting to tear up as they listened to me. That set me off.

'The amazing thing about John …'

My voice started to catch and I knew that I was going to start crying myself. I took a deep breath and tried to compose myself enough to carry on, ignoring the tear rolling down my cheek.

'The amazing thing about John was that, although I treated him this way, he was the most caring and kind-hearted brother. If I had been fortunate to have drug awareness education or support to deal with this problem, I would have known how to treat him in the way he deserved.'

I needed people to hear that message: this is what happens when you make drug use a criminal offence and it's time to accept that it simply hasn't worked.

Growing up, our parents tell us not to take drugs and yet we still have drug addicts. The government tells us we can't take drugs and we still do it. Would it not be better to change the message? Keep educating people – it's wrong to take drugs, and this is all of the damage that they will do to you – but let people know that if you do make that really bad choice in life and you do take drugs, don't worry, there's a way back from that. John was pushed so far out to the fringes of society that he never found his way home again. He made a mistake and lived with the consequences for the rest of his short life.

To anyone who has an addict in their family, don't be embarrassed. I couldn't even listen to John when he tried to make a joke at the dinner table; my reaction shut down the lines of communication between us when he needed somebody the most. Instead, talk to someone that can educate you on how to deal with the problem. Don't judge and don't let others judge. Realise that everybody in this world makes mistakes. Understand that addiction is a mental health issue. Life is not perfect. Your family is not perfect. Nobody's is.

I didn't want to talk to anybody about John's addiction when I was younger, not to Steo, not to Davey, not to my girlfriend at the time, not to my parents. I wanted to hide it. I wanted to bottle it up. But I know that when I did start speaking about it in recent years, I felt a weight off my shoulders. I felt proud that I could speak about the troubles that my brother went through. How brave would it be if a teenager could do what I couldn't, could stand up in front of his friends and say, 'My brother is a drug addict and I'm going to help him'? How powerful would that message be? It's a very hard thing to ask anyone to do, but only because we hide from our problems and try to project this image of a perfect life; we try to push our negativity on to other people, we try to make ourselves feel better by making others feel worse.

My parents told John not to take drugs. Did it stop him? No, and I believe there was very little that you could have said to him that would have stopped him, unless he saw someone struggling first-hand for himself. I didn't take drugs because I saw the mistakes he made and the pain that he went through because of them. Bring your kids into Mountjoy on school trips, show them what's happening to drug addicts, show them a video of somebody dying from drugs, give them this book, tell them John's story. That's the best way you can discourage them from taking drugs. The education that we're giving to our kids at the moment is clearly not working because we still have addicts in this country, and if we keep going down the road, we will for generations. We'll never get rid of it.

I grew up going to funerals. Families all over Ireland are still losing their loved ones, one addict dying every day in stairwells and on streets because we can't deal with the problem, and we haven't even seen the damage that a crack cocaine or crystal meth epidemic would do. Is this country equipped for when dealers start bringing in more and more of another one of these dangerous drugs? Not a hope.

There are more people in the country smoking cigarettes than there are using heroin, and smoking causes more deaths than heroin each year. Logically, the nicotine in the cigarettes is killing more people than the heroin, and while we'll sell you as many packets of cigarettes as you want in the local shop, if you touch heroin you're the lowest of the low. A junkie – that disgusting, dehumanising word. That is the meaning that our society has put on drug addiction. It's damaging, it's passed down from generation to generation, and we accept it without thinking and it hasn't changed. What if it's wrong?

I'm not advocating that we make a dangerous drug like heroin freely available, but there's a big difference between legalisation and decriminalisation. Decriminalisation isn't really about the drug, it's about decriminalising the human being in question and changing the stigma. And if you don't do that, the only person who wins is the drug dealer. They are the ones making all the money while the guards and the government are more focused on picking up drug addicts off the streets and arresting them. The right thing to do is to cut addicts out of the market by designating them as mental health cases, and instead of spending millions of euro on incarcerating them, spend the money on mandatory recovery programmes.

We've got to realise that homelessness, drug addiction, and mental health, the three big problem areas in 21st-century Ireland, are all interlinked, but we wait until we have a crisis in our country before we do anything. We wait until there are people dying outside the Dáil before we accept that homelessness is getting worse, not better. We wait until we have the third highest overdose rate in Europe before we rethink our drugs strategy. We wait until mental health becomes an epidemic before we finally start to open up and talk to each other. Why are we so reactive?

I have met politicians who are out there fighting for better drug policies: Catherine Byrne, Aodhán Ó Ríordáin, Lynn Ruane. A lot of the time, politics comes down to one thing: how much do you care? In any walk of life, you need to have an emotional connection to your professional goal, otherwise it's too easy to get despondent and give up when people start pushing back against you. I'm not saying we need to elect drug addicts in order to fight for better policies, but we need people who won't take no for an answer.

I was down in a school in Navan to give a talk one day. Helen McEntee, who was the Minister of State for Mental Health and Older People at the time, was speaking as well. She was elected in 2013 after her father took his own life. I could see how focused and driven she was and I thought, 'That's what this country needs, people that are really connected with their job.' She really cares. Do we have enough politicians who are like her? Do we have enough politicians that are so dissatisfied that, no matter what, their vision and the practical work they can do will always overcome any resistance they meet? I don't know.

Bringing in supervised injection clinics is a step in the right direction, because taking drugs off the streets will go a long way towards reducing the stigma. There won't be as many needles on the streets or in the places where children play; there won't be as many people lying on the streets goofing off; and people will have less reason to be afraid around addicts. Opponents will claim that it normalises drugs, that it lets people stay on drugs, but it doesn't. It brings them together in one area where you can target them for recovery rather than leaving them scattered around the city homeless. You want to take drugs? We're going to watch you, we're going to make sure that you're safe, that you're not going to die, and that you've a longer time to stay on the planet to become a recovered addict. The alternative is to just leave them on the streets to die, which is essentially what the previous policies have done.

In Portugal, drugs are decriminalised in small quantities and rightly seen as a harm, not a crime. Instead of shutting the door on addicts, they are referred to a panel made up of a doctor, a judge, and a social worker, who can set them a recovery programme and a way back into society. They might not always become clean, but at least society is making a positive effort to help them rather than casting them aside. It prevents what happened to my family from happening over and over again. Families don't become embarrassed about the addict in their lives. They see that there's a problem there, no different to someone that's struggling with depression, and that the right thing to do is to talk about it and find a way to treat it.

I am not an expert in drugs, but I am an expert in having a family member who was a drug addict and you can't argue with that. The traditional policies in this country certainly haven't helped me or my family, and there's no question that they didn't help John.

———

Every time I walk out onto the pitch, John is right there with me, reminding me to cherish every moment of this incredible adventure. Ben Farrell is an inspiration to me too. How many five-year-olds can you say that about?

I only met Ben once. He came down to the Dublin training base with his mam and dad, Alan and Valerie, and his little brother and his friend. To look at him, you would never know that this kid was in the middle of the fight of his life. He had so much energy, running around, jumping over walls, and getting up to all sorts, and I couldn't believe that this was the same little boy who had been through more courses of chemotherapy and radiation therapy than you could begin to imagine. He just lit up the room.

Ben was diagnosed with an extremely rare form of cancer at Christmas 2015. After trying every possible option here in

Ireland, Alan and Valerie wanted to bring him to America where there was a new treatment that could potentially save his life. The cost was huge, but they managed to raise an incredible amount of money, and we were happy to get publicity and lend them support in whatever little way we could. Ben was a massive Dubs fan – it was the least we could do.

People all over Ireland got to know Ben and his story. He was Batman Ben, who loved dressing up in his mask and a black cape. He was a brilliant young lad, way smarter than his age, and had an incredible happiness and sense of humour in spite of everything that he was going through.

Ben was Trevor Croly's nephew and Trevor told a story which summed him up perfectly. When he started his treatment in Crumlin, Ben noticed that there was a big red button beside his bed. When he asked the nurse what it was for, she told him that it was only for emergencies. That was a good enough explanation for Ben. A few minutes later, the alarm went off and when the nurse came running back in to see what the emergency was, Ben was smiling away.

'I just wanted to tell you that I love you,' he said.

Ben sadly died a few days before we played Kerry in the 2016 All-Ireland semi-final. I know he would have loved to be there to cheer us on, and then to celebrate with us afterwards. I couldn't get him out of my head when I went up to training that night. I said a few words to the lads as I told them the news, that this little kid who was bouncing around our changing room only a few weeks earlier had passed away. He had to put up with so much suffering and so much pain in his short life and he did it like the superhero that he was.

'Look, lads,' I said, 'we're lucky. We're all able to go out and train tonight. We're able to put a jersey on and run out onto the pitch and kick a football. Remember that.'

I know Ben was in my head when we went out to play Kerry the following week, and knowing the lads that are in that dressing room with me, I'm sure he was in some of their heads too. That's what spiritual motivation is on the football pitch, the inspiration that pushes you further or that picks you up when you fall. That tackle, that block, that run, that bad pass you made, whatever it is that you want to move on from so that you can focus on the next challenge – that's when you look to someone like John to pick you up, and Ben was right there beside him that day.

The Dublin fans paid Ben a brilliant tribute by arranging a minute's applause for him in the fifth minute. On the pitch, we paid our own tribute in the only way we could, by leaving it all out there and winning the game.

When I went back into the dressing room afterwards, I had brought a Batman T-shirt with me in my gearbag. I put it on and tweeted out a photo with the message: 'The little Batman was watching over us!'

He was. Thanks, buddy.

———

In 2015, when I brought that new, attacking side to my game, it got people's attention. That was the year I won my first All-Star and I was nominated for Footballer of the Year, but you can't change your game like that every year, you can't always do something that's so obviously different to what's gone before. But it's funny because, defensively, I actually felt that I had a better season in 2016. That summer I marked some of the top forwards in the country: Donie Kingston, Mickey Newman, John Heslin, Michael Murphy, Kieran Donaghy, and Cillian

O'Connor. Only one of them managed to score more than a point from play off me – O'Connor got two in the drawn All-Ireland final, but I held him scoreless in the replay.

Those two All-Ireland finals against Mayo in 2016 were two more savage battles. We've had a lot of them over the last few seasons. I stood and watched O'Connor line up that last free into the Hill 16 end and already I was thinking about the next kickout. Where did I need to be? I would have put my house on him putting it over the bar to equalise, and once he did, I knew Clucko would try to take the restart as quickly as possible. I wasn't thinking about the prospect of him missing, or of a fourth All-Ireland medal. I was thinking about what I had to do to win the next ball.

In all of my years playing for Dublin, my number one goal has never changed – to get that blue jersey and to wear it as many times as possible. I put everything I can into achieving that. Anything that comes after it has been the most remarkable bonus, beyond the wildest of my wildest dreams.

The success is only as important as the people that you're able to share it with. All of my Dublin medals – O'Byrne Cup, League, Leinster, and All-Ireland – go straight to Mam. If she hasn't seen me or the medal for a couple of days after we win, I know I can expect a phone call.

'Where's my medal, Philip? I need it for the wall.'

Every single one of them is framed along with my jersey from that season, signed by all of my teammates, the men I went to war with, and they take pride of place in her sitting room, alongside the photo of my first ever win in Croke Park with the Holy Spirit hurling team all those years ago.

Dad doesn't get any medals, but he likes to take Sam out for a walk around the neighbourhood if I take my eye off it for a second. I'll be in the kitchen chatting to Mam, or upstairs getting ready, and by the time I come back down to grab the cup and go, it will have disappeared. He never goes too far, but you might have to knock on a few doors of a few different houses before you'll find him in among a pile of neighbours and their kids, everybody striking their best championship pose as they get their picture taken.

Or the two of us will be out for a walk, and he'll stop to chat to someone he knows. People never need to ask me for a photo if they meet me and I'm with Dad; he'll always ask them if they want one first, before they've even had a chance.

And before they leave, 'Make sure you drop that jersey over to me as well and Philly will get it signed for you.'

That's how proud Mam and Dad are of me. I just hope they know that everything I've done, everything that I've achieved, it's all thanks to them.

I never got a chance to share any of it with John. We went out that night after beating Mayo and celebrated winning back-to-back All-Irelands, something that no Dublin team had done since the 1970s. It's hard not to think about how much he would have loved to be there, in the thick of the party and the drinking and the messing. I know I would have had to drag him away from it all at the end of the night, the last man standing, still telling anybody who would listen about how great I had played and how proud he was to be my brother.

There's no point in being a Dublin footballer, no point in having all of the businesses and money, if you're not content with what you have in your life. It means absolutely nothing. I'd give all the money I have, and all the money I'd make in the future, and all of the All-Irelands to still have John here today. Life is not about what you have. It's about finding happiness with the people who are closest to you.

———

My Half Time Talk changed my life. Now I want everybody in Ireland to have a Half Time Talk. I want the country to have a Half Time Talk.

When the government funding for the Kaizen Evolution fitness course in Ballymun fell through, I started to work on other ways that I could continue to provide that social support to 18–24s in the area. One idea was to set up an institute that would train people to become certified fitness instructors, probably with a view to opening their own gym down the line. When those people paid their fees, part of the money would go towards covering our operating costs, and the rest would go towards creating a fund in John's name – The John Caffrey Scholarship – which would cover the tuition fees for at-risk youths who wanted to take the course themselves.

Then that idea evolved again. I was getting so many phone calls, from schools, charities, youth clubs, community organisations, and businesses. They all wanted me to come and speak to them and share my story, and no matter how many of them I was able to say yes to, there were always more I had to turn down. I hated that. These were organisations and causes that I would love to help, but every time I turned around and said, 'No, sorry, I don't have time,' I felt that I was letting people down. I couldn't create more hours in the day for myself, so I did something that would allow me to help as many people as possible with the time I had. I decided to set up a charity.

Standing up in front of people and telling them my story forced me to think about my life and why I did the things I did. When I talked about my life, I always broke it down into two very different parts – before John died, and after John died. The beauty of the Half Time Talk as a concept is that it tells my specific story perfectly, but at the same time, it can apply to anyone, at any stage of their life. It's a powerful tool.

After a bit of thought, I knew what I wanted the charity to be. I had the blueprint from the Kaizen Evolution course, and from the original plans for the fitness institute, but I didn't want this charity to run its own courses or set up a scholarship fund. If it did that, it might only be able to impact a couple of hundred people a year, which would be brilliant, but I wanted to do so much more. Besides, there are enough organisations out there in Ireland who already have that expertise and structure and are doing an excellent job of that. What I wanted to do with Half Time Talk is to make sure that they have the financial support to run their programmes – the support that the Ballymun–Whitehall Area Partnership was missing when we wanted to do a second year in Ballymun. These kinds of organisations cannot afford to be reliant on government funding. If these training and development courses are going to be the Half Time Talk of people's lives, I want to make sure that anybody who wants to participate gets that opportunity.

By working with leaders in local communities, the charity will help identify ways to tackle community issues and connect with young people who need help. Everyone should be able to develop life skills, to work on their self-belief and self-image, and to get the support to change their lives for their better. By building the charity around local heroes and the needs of individual communities, I hope that Half Time Talk will ultimately support hundreds, if not thousands, of courses across Ireland and shape our country for the better.

Everything has to start from somewhere, but my vision is that in two or three years' time, everybody will know what a Half Time Talk is, and everyone that wants to access one of our courses will be able to do it. I want people to walk away from us and be proud to say 'I've had a Half Time Talk', and for it to mean something, for employers to come on board with us and get our participants into work, to recognise the adversity that these people have overcome in their lives just to get to this point and see the value that they can bring to a business, whatever that may be.

As I write this, I've already spent more than a year building Half Time Talk as a charity, recruiting a really strong board of directors to help, and developing the charity's strategy and governance with a larger advisory board. If all goes according to plan, the first Half Time Talk pilot scheme is due to begin in late 2017.

Like everything in my life, it will start in Ballymun.

# Epilogue
## 1 October 2016

I couldn't miss the headstone. The big crests of the three teams that you loved – Everton, Celtic, and the Dubs. I can only imagine the laugh you would have if you could see people nudge and point as they walked past.

'Look at that one over there, an Everton fan.'

The grave looks well. Fresh flowers and the weeds have been pulled. Mam must have been up recently.

I don't always come up here before a match, but I try to do it as much as I can. The cemetery is quiet today, a few bits and pieces of conversation, the sound of feet on the gravel, but other than that it's just the planes either taking off or coming in to land up the road. It's perfect.

The rest of the day will be planned down to the minute with military precision. Out onto the pitch for the warm up: 4.29pm. Pre-match parade: 4.52pm. '*Amhrán na bhFiann*': 4.58pm.

For these few minutes though, my time is still my own, before the headphones go on and I head to join the rest of the team and everything else is blocked out from my world. Now I can be alone with my thoughts.

I stop at the grave and I have a few words. I know that you can't hear me, John, but just by getting in the car and driving up here to think about you, even if it's only for a few minutes, it feels like we're spending a little bit of time together again. Brothers.

I think about all of the good things in my life that you would be excited to hear about, and all of the things in your life that I wish you felt able to talk to me about. If you were here, I'd bring you with me everywhere. I'd show you that I wasn't embarrassed by you, that I was proud of you and the adversity that you had come through, even if your fight wasn't over.

I'd show you the other side of life, all the positive things that we could share together, and that you could have for yourself.

I'd get you to chase a dream of your own. Train up for an amateur MMA fight, maybe. Work your way up to manage one of the gyms. Get one of your poems published.

I'd get you to talk to people, tell them your story, and to realise the good that talking could do to help you and to help others who are struggling.

Choice is the most powerful thing that any one of us has in our lives. Big choices, little choices. Choices with massive consequences and choices with none. Sometimes we make good choices and sometimes we make bad ones.

I am who I am because of your choices, John. I saw your mistakes and your pain, and they pushed me the other way.

If you were still here, I would be a totally different person, living my life on autopilot, not realising what true happiness is all about. I would never have found the spiritual motivation I have now that drives me to savour my football, to achieve in business, to be a better person. But we all have the choice to be grateful and appreciative and to strive for a better second half in life. We don't need to wait for something bad to happen.

I don't want your legacy to be the life that you lost at the age of 31. It's because of you that I want to help people; I want to live your legacy for you. I sometimes think that if you had known what would happen – that you would struggle with addiction and die at such a young age, but that when you died I would work to save hundreds of thousands of lives in your name – you would have snapped at it.

There's a reason why I come up to the graveyard on the morning of a big match. It reminds me how lucky I am to be part of such a talented group of players, to be able to go out and play the game I love for a team that means the world to me. It is a privilege that I will never, ever take for granted.

I love sport and I love being a winner, but what I love more is the profile that allows me to go out and make a difference to someone else's day or someone else's life. The world has so much negativity, hurt and anger. I've come to realise that you get one shot at life, so why not leave a legacy behind and have people remember you for doing something positive? People might remember certain footballers for 5 or 10 years, but people will remember someone who helped others for maybe 20, 30, 40 years or, even better, they will take inspiration from that person's work and pass it on to the next generation.

It's not about trying to save the world, it's about doing whatever is in your capacity. It's about waking up in the morning and being positive about the day that's ahead of you, not only seeing the challenges but seeing the opportunities as well. It's about finding that little kid and sitting down on the path beside him to give him a little bit of help and encouragement, and doing that as many times as you can with as many people as you can. It's about showing compassion and respect to the people all around us, especially the ones who are fighting battles that we will never truly understand. That is the choice that we all have every single day.

A quick glance at my watch. I'd better go, the bus will be waiting. Anyway, I'll talk to you soon, John. We've got work to do, me and you.